AMERICAN CITIES CHRONOLOGY SERIES

DETROIT

A CHRONOLOGICAL & DOCUMENTARY HISTORY

1701-1976

Compiled and Edited by
ROBERT I. VEXLER

Series Editor
HOWARD B. FURER

1977
OCEANA PUBLICATIONS, INC.
Dobbs Ferry, New York

To my family

Library of Congress Cataloging in Publication Data

Main entry under title:

Detroit: a chronological & documentary history,
1701-1976.

(American cities chronology series)
Bibliography: p.
Includes index.
SUMMARY: A chronology of major events in Detroit's history with pertinent documents included.
1. Detroit — History — Chronology. 2. Detroit — History — Sources. I. Vexler, Robert I.
F574.D457D48 977.4'34 77-9375
ISBN 0-379-00605-7

Manufactured in the United States of America

TABLE OF CONTENTS

EDITOR'S FOREWORD

Every effort has been made to cite the most accurate dates in the Chronology. Various newspapers, documents, and letters and chronicles have been consulted to verify this information or to change dates when proven plausible.

Because the very nature of preparing a chronology of this type precludes the author from using the standard form of historical footnoting, I should like to acknowledge in this editor's foreword the major sources used to compile the bulk of the chronological and factual materials comprising the chronology section of this work. They are as follows: Clarence M. Burton, The City of Detroit, Michigan, 1701-1922, 4 vols.; George B. Catlin, The Story of Detroit; Detroit Public Library, Rae Elizabeth Rips, ed. Detroit In Its World Setting; A 250-Year Chronology, 1701-1951; Silas Farmer, The History of Detroit and Michigan; Ferris E. Lewis, Detroit; A Wilderness Outpost of Old France; and Arthur Pound, Detroit, Dynamic City.

This research tool is compiled primarily for the student. The importance of political, social, economic and cultural events have been evaluated in relation to their significance. Detroit has played a major role in the development of the United States. Its position on Lake Erie enabled its citizens to recognize the potential for trade and industry. Detroit was able to reform its political system and to improve upon its governance during the early twentieth century. The development of the automobile industry enabled it to grow in size and importance in the nation. It was the largest city to recall a mayor in 1930. Detroit initiated a program of urban redevelopment after the Second World War. It was believed that many of its race problems had been settled in the years after the 1943 riot, but it was to discover that the tensions had grown beneath the surface when they erupted in the July riot in 1967. Since then further reforms and reconstruction have begun.

Documents have been selected which best illustrate the major aspects in the development of Detroit from the small town under French and British rule to the bustling and growing city of the 1960's.

Robert I. Vexler
Briarcliff College

EARLY DETROIT

1701 June 2. Antoine de La Mothe Cadillac left Montreal for the Detroit River.

July 4. Cadillac and his soldiers and traders landed at the site of Detroit.

July 26. St. Anne's Day was celebrated with a service, which was the beginning of plans for building St. Anne's Church.

October 7. The first wheat was planted in Wayne County.

1703 The Indians burned the Church and other buildings.

May 30. The first women, Madame Cadillac and Madame de Tonty, arrived at Detroit.

1704 February 2. Marie Therese Cadillac was baptised. This was the first baptism in Detroit.

1706 June 26. The Indians attacked the Fort.

1707 March 10. Cadillac made the first known grants of land.

August 6-10. A council of Indian chiefs was held at Fort Ponchartrain (Detroit) to settle Indian difficulties.

1708 A new church was built, but it was burned in 1712 to prevent the attacking Indians from using it.

1710 Cadillac was appointed Governor of Louisiana. He left Detroit in the summer of 1711 and never returned.

May 5. Jean Baptiste Turpin and Margaret Fufard were the first white couple married at Detroit.

1712 Jacques Charles Sabrevois was appointed commandant of the fort.

The Sioux and Fox Indians attacked Fort Pontchartrain. The Huron and Ottawa Indians aided the settlers in defeating the attackers.

1723 The third Catholic church building was erected. It was the first named St. Anne's.

1729 Robert Navarre arrived from France as Intendant to conduct civil affairs.

1734 A dam was built across Cacacier's Creek, and a grist mill was erected to grind flour.

1746 The Indians attacked the Fort.

1749 Joseph de Lery, an engineer, drew up a plan of Detroit.

1752 A famine and smallpox epidemic occurred at Detroit.

1755 Many Acadians who were banished from Nova Scotia were given refuge in Detroit.

1758 Francois Picoté de Bellestre was appointed commandant.

1760 November 29. Detroit was occupied by Major Robert Rogers and English troops according to the peace terms with France of September, 1760.

1761 A plot by the Seneca and Huron Indians to massacre the garrison at Detroit was frustrated by quick action. Sir William Johnson and others arrived on September 3, 1761 with Major Henry Gladwin. He remained through 1762, and Gladwin became commandant in July, 1762.

1763 May 10. Pontiac's Indian followers attacked Detroit. The siege lasted until October 31, when the Indians were finally turned back.

July 29. Captain Dalzell arrived from New England to raise the siege of Detroit.

1764 April 27. Zion Lodge of the Masons, No. 1, was founded at Detroit by the warrant of George Harrison, Grand Master of the province of New York.

August 31. Major Gladwin turned over command of the Fort to Colonel John Bradstreet who had arrived August 26. Captain George Campbell became commandant in the Fall.

1766 The Indian Chief Pontiac and Sir William

Johnson met at Fort Ontario and reached an agreement in which Pontiac gave his allegiance to the British.

1768 May 26. Philippe de Jean was elected judge in the first election at Detroit.

1770 September. Captain James Stephenson became commandant.

1772 Fall. Major Henry Bassett became commandant.

1774 June 22. The British passed the Quebec Act which placed Detroit under the civil administration of England.

November 9. Henry Hamilton became commandant.

1775 April. Detroit was annexed to Quebec.

1778 Fort Lerroult was added to Fort Pontchartrain.

March. Daniel Boone was held captive by the Indians in Detroit.

1779 October. Major Arent Schuyler took command of Detroit.

1781 November. Moravian teachers came to Detroit. They opened a trail to their settlement at Mt. Clemens in 1782.

1783 July 4. Major Ephraim Douglass, first representative of the United States government, entered Detroit.

September 3. The United States and England signed the peace treaty. Detroit was included in the public domain of the United States.

1784 Spring. Major William Ancrum took charge of Detroit.

1786 Captain Thomas Bennett became commandant.

1788 July 24. Detroit was included in the Canadian district of Hesse by the British. The town was under British and Canadian law, despite the United States Northwest Ordinance of 1787. The British continued to claim the territory until 1796.

1791 December 26. Detroit and Michigan were incorporated in Upper Canada.

1792 Summer. Colonel Richard England became the last English commandant of Detroit.

1793 Joseph Roe taught school until 1797.

William Macomb bought Belle Isle from George and Robert MacDougal.

1794 Matthew Donoval began to teach school and continued until 1798 or 1799.

1795 June 16. The orphans court was established.

1796 Catholic jurisdiction over Detroit passed from the Bishop of Quebec to the Bishop of Baltimore after the United States and Britain agreed that the former owned the territory.

January 29. The final sitting of an English court of General Quarter Sessions occurred at Detroit.

July 11. The British evacuated Detroit and turned it over to the United States. The American flag was raised for the first time at noon.

July 13. Colonel John Francis Hamtramck arrived in Detroit as its commander.

August 13. General Anthony Wayne arrived in Detroit and established army headquarters.

August 15. Wayne County was organized in the Northwest Territory. It was named for General Wayne.

October 8. The first American Court of Quarter Sessions met at Detroit.

December. The Court of Quarter Sessions divided Wayne County into four townships including Detroit.

1798 The town acquired its first hand fire engine and established a number of cisterns in various places to supply water for the engine.

December 17. Detroit held its first election

for delegates to the Northwest Territory General Assembly. Solomon Sibley was chosen.

1799 March 2. Detroit was made a port of entry by Act of congress.

1800 May. Peter Joseph Dillon opened a school.

September 11. Rev. David Bacon, Protestant missionary, arrived.

December 9. A Circuit Court of Wayne County was authorized to be held on the third Tuesday of May in each year.

1801 Police constables were appointed for the first time.

March. The first post road in Michigan from Detroit to Cincinnati was opened, but it was discontinued three years later when a road from Cleveland was established.

May 25. Rev. David Bacon began teaching school. Mrs. Bacon opened a school for girls shortly after this date.

INCORPORATION OF DETROIT

1802 Mail service with Washington was begun. Charles Curry became the first postmaster at Detroit.

January 18. Governor Arthur St. Clair approved the measure incorporating the town of Detroit. The charter named five trustees: John Askin, John Dodemead, James Henry, Charles F. Girardin and Joseph Campau.

February 23. An ordinance was adopted requiring that all chimneys be swept every two weeks between October and April and every four weeks the rest of the year, which was a part of the regulations for fire prevention.

April 17. The first city tax totalling $150 was assessed, charging each individual over 21, a sum of 25 cents. A tax on houses was also enacted.

May 3. The first municipal election was held.

September 7. Frederick Bates was appointed postmaster.

1803 April 11. When John F. Hamtramck died, Major Zebulon Pike became commandant of the military post.

1804 The first Protestant mssionary to the white people of Detroit, Nathaniel Bangs, a Methodist, arrived.

A dock ordinance was passed to build a new wharf, because the old one was in a state of decay.

A patrol, including a night watch, was established.

Father Richard opened the Young Ladies' Academy and began a class for boys to develop an interest in the priesthood.

A nightwatch was established to protect the citizens from the Indians.

March 16. President Jefferson approved an act setting apart section 16 in each township for educational purposes.

March 26. The United States land office was established in Detroit

1805 January 11. The Territory of Michigan was created out of Indiana Territory with Detroit as the capital.

June 11. Detroit was completely destroyed by fire.

June 30. The federal government established a government of a Governor and Judges for Detroit and the Territory. Men were then appointed to office who did not understand the city.

July 1. The citizens adopted a tentative plan for a new town modeled on the old one which had been destroyed.

August 19. The first session of the Michigan Territorial government was held at Richard Smyth's tavern.

THE CITY OF DETROIT

1806 September 13. The Governor and Judges passed an act incorporating the City of Detroit. They also gave permission to Hull and Woodward to lay out the new city.

September 19. The Bank of Detroit, created by act of the Governor and Judges of Michigan Territory, was opened.

October. John Goff opened a school.

1807 November 17. Governor Hull of the Michigan Territory held a council at Detroit with the chiefs of the Chippewa, Pottawatomi and Wyandot tribes, which led to the conclusion of a treaty ceding much territory to the United States.

1808 Francois Paul Malcher granted his farm to Catholic trustees for religion and education.

1809 Father Gabriel Richard introduced the first printing press into Detroit.

February 26. Judge James Witherall drew up an education bill for Michigan Territory.

August 1. The Childs Spelling Book, or Michigan Instructor was issued. It was a small 12-page speller.

August 31. The Michigan Essay, or Impartial Observer was issued as the first newspaper in Detroit, and first Catholic paper in English in the United States. Only one issue is in existence today.

1810 The Methodist Society established the first Protestant Church group under Rev. William Mitchell.

Daniel Curtis began teaching in Detroit and continued until the Summer of 1812.

1812 August 16. Detroit surrendered to the British under Major General Isaac Brock. This was part of the War of 1812.

1813 September 10. Commodore Oliver H. Perry's fleet defeated the British on Lake Erie.

September 29. Detroit was recaptured by American troops.

October. A cholera-like epidemic occurred killing many.

1814 September 10. The Indians attacked Detroit, but they were soon forced to withdraw.

1815 September 15. The first Evangelistic Society of Detroit was organized.

October 24. Governor Lewis Cass approved an act granting a new charter to Detroit, and restoring control of local affairs to the people. Five trustees were to be elected to serve until the first Monday in May, 1816, after which date annual elections for officers were to be held.

December 29. The Moral and Humane Society was established as the first charitable organization in the city.

1816 April 18. A Peace Treaty was concluded with the Indian Council, including Tecumseh's brother, "The Prophet."

June 10. The old engine belonging to Commodore Perry's ship was purchased for use by a fire company.

1817 William Brookfield and his wife conducted a school.

July 25. The first number of the Detroit Gazette was issued. The last number appeared April 22, 1830.

August 13. President James Monroe came to Detroit for a five-day visit.

August 26. The Territorial government passed an act appropriating $380 for the establishment of the University of Michigan.

The City Library Society was incorporated.

September 8. The University of Michigan was organized.

November 3. Mr. Banvard opened a school at the Council House.

December 19. The Bank of Michigan was incorporated. It ended its business in 1869.

December 29. The Moral and Humane Society was founded.

1818 Edwin Baldwin established a regular ferry service between Detroit and Windsor--first by canoe and then by rowboat.

A number of ladies organized the "Ladies' Society of Detroit" for charitable purposes.

January 14. The Lyceum of the City of Detroit was organized. Its constitution was adopted June 29.

July 27. An ordinance was passed providing for public whipping of drunkards, disorderly persons, petty thieves, wife-beaters and other small offenders.

August. The first steamship, the Walk-in-the-Water, arrived.

September 20. A treaty was signed with the Ottawa and Wyandotte Indians, which included a grant of land to the Catholic Church of St. Anne and the College of Detroit.

November. Antoine Dequindré was given permission to build the first sewer.

1819 The citizens voted a tax levy to buy a more modern fire engine, although it was not obtained until six years later.

June 14. An act was passed which authorized the physicians and surgeons to meet in Detroit on July 3 to form a medical society.

1820 The population of Detroit was 1,422.

The first post roads were established from Detroit to Pontiac and Mt. Clements.

1821 April 21. The first Methodist Society was organized.

April 30. The original act establishing the University of Michigan was repealed, and it was reorganized.

May. E. W. Godwin opened a private school, and T. Young established an English school.

November. Mr. and Mrs. Brookfield opened the "seminary" school.

1822 The Female Benevolent Society of Detroit was organized.

Public stages began running from Detroit.

March 21. The first Methodist Episcopal Society of Detroit was organized.

June. A stage coach route opened between Detroit and Mt. Clemens.

1823 August 5. Peter Berthelet was authorized to build a wharf and install a pump to take water from the river, where it would be free from shore contamination. This grant was for 99 years.

October 27. The University trustees voted to permit Mr. Carpenter to occupy a room in the university building for a school.

1824 Mr. Shepard conducted a primary school in a small building at the University. Mrs. Shepard opened a female school in May, 1825.

Mr. Wells and three associates were granted exclusive right to supply water to the city until 1850. They formed the Hydraulic Company.

June 7. The first legislative Council of Michigan Territory met in Detroit.

August 5. A new City Charter was granted which established the offices of mayor, recorder, as well as a common council of five members. A special election was to be held on the first Monday in September, and the officers were to serve until the first regular election on the first Monday in April, 1825.

September 6. John R. Williams was elected Mayor.

September 21. The first session of the Common Council was held.

November 22. The first Episcopal Church in Detroit, St. Paul's, was incorporated.

1825 January 23. The First Presbyterian Church was organized.

February. Bethel Farrand was authorized to put a new water works system into operation. He built it with Rufus Wells.

The first Episcopal Church was established.

April. Henry J. Hunt was elected Mayor.

May 10. The Michigan Herald, a Whig weekly paper, first appeared. Its last number was published April 30, 1829.

September 21. Fire Engine No. 1 was purchased.

October 31. The Gazette Francais, first French paper published in the territory, was first issued and continued for three months.

1826 When the federal troops left the fort it was donated to the city along with the Military Reserve by Congress.

April. Jonathan Kearsley was elected Mayor.

1827 The Mansion House Hotel was opened.

The first steamboat, The Argo, was built at Detroit for use as a ferry boat.

The first Baptist Church was organized.

Eagle Fire Company No. 2 was organized.

March. The Common Council granted Rufus Wells sole right to supply the city with water. The pump house erected had a capacity of 9,500 gallons.

April 4. A new City Charter was granted under the following name: "The Mayor, Recorder, Aldermen and Freemen of the City of Detroit."

April. John Biddle was elected Mayor.

April 12. An act establishing "common schools" was passed. The first school was opened in June.

November 26. The City Council passed an ordinance requiring sidewalks. They were originally built of wooden planks.

1828 April 7. John Biddle was reelected Mayor.

May 5. The State Capitol Building was opened, and served as such until the capital was moved to Lansing in 1847.

June 23. The Historical Society of Michigan was incorporated by Lewis Cass, Henry R. Schoolcraft, and others.

November 14. P. W. Heady was given permission to open a school in the University Building.

1829 The _Tribune_, a Whig weekly paper was founded. It merged with the _News_ in 1915.

April. Jonathan Kearsley was elected Mayor.

November 20. _The Northwestern Journal_, a weekly, was first published. Its name was changed to _The Detroit Journal and Michigan Advertiser_ on November 24, 1830. On March 1, 1833, the paper was called _The Detroit Journal_ and was published semi-weekly. It later became the _Detroit Journal and Courier_ and then the _Journal and Advertiser._

1830 February 19. The first city temperance society was organized.

March 18. The Detroit Female Seminary was incorporated.

April. John R. Williams was elected Mayor.

July 31. The Detroit and Pontiac Railroad was chartered. Its charter was ended, and in 1834 another charter was granted to a new corporation also named the Detroit and Pontiac Railroad.

September 24. Stephen G. Simmons was hanged for murdering his wife in Detroit. This was the last execution in Michigan.

December 6. The Lyceum of Michigan, a library, was organized, and lasted about one year.

December 23. The Detroit Courier was established. It merged with The Detroit Journal in January, 1835 and appeared as The Detroit Journal and Courier on January 21, 1835. It appeared semi-weekly in February, 1835.

1831 Alexis de Tocqueville visited Detroit.

January 9. Mail service began between Detroit and the East.

April. Marshall Chapin was elected Mayor.

May 5. The first number of The Democratic Free Press and Michigan Intelligencer appeared. It was a weekly until May 19, 1835 and then became a semi-weekly. It finally became a daily on September 28, 1835. It began publishing a weekly edition in London in 1881 and was the only American paper in Europe for two years.

July 15. The Detroit Atheneum was organized to maintain a reading room and club. It merged into the Detroit Young Men's Society in 1836.

1832 April. Levi Cook was elected Mayor.

June 29. The Detroit and St. Joseph Railroad was chartered.

July. A cholera epidemic began.

1833 The Chicago Road was completed.

The Roman Catholic Diocese of Detroit was established. Saint Anne's became the Cathedral Church and Frederick Resé came to Detroit as the first Bishop.

The Wolverine Fire Company No. 2 was founded.

The Howell Medical Act was passed providing for registration of all who practiced medicine.

January. The Wayne County Poorhouse opened.

January 13. The Detroit Young Men's Society

was formally organized.

April. Marshall Chapin was elected Mayor.

April 22. The City Charter was amended authorizing the first city taxes on real and personal property.

June. The Sisters of St. Claire Seminary of Pittsburgh opened a school in Detroit.

June 14-15. A Negro riot occurred to prevent Thornton Blackburn, a runaway slave, from being returned to Kentucky officials. He was taken to Canada where he was arrested, but the Canadian government would not surrender him to the Kentuckians.

August 1. D. B. Crane opened a high school.

August 18. The first Lutheran Church, St. John's German Evangelical Church, was opened.

September. Mr. Olds opened a writing school.

December 2. The Michigan High School opened.

1834 Major McKinstry opened the "Michigan Garden," a public garden.

The College of St. Philip Neri was established.

The Catholic Female Association was organized "for the relief of the sick and poor."

April. Charles C. Trowbridge was elected Mayor. Andrew Mack served as Mayor later in the year.

May 13. Major David McKinstry's museum was opened to the public.

August - September. Detroit suffered a second cholera epidemic.

October. The Mechanics' Academy was opened.

1835 The city streets were lighted by twenty sperm oil lamps. Naptha lamps were used in 1877.

The first systematic street paving began.

April. Levi Cook was elected Mayor.

May 11. The first state constitutional convention met in Detroit. The Constitution drawn up, was approved by the voters on October 5.

September 28. The Daily Free Press, the first daily paper, was issued.

November 3. Stevens T. Mason was inaugurated as the first Governor of Michigan.

November 18. The first City Hall was occupied.

1836 The National Hotel and the American Hotel were opened.

The Sixteen Mile House opened. It was later named Botsford Tavern.

The city purchased the Hydraulic Company Waterworks and began operating it.

The city government ordered the placement of street names at street corners.

The Allegheny and Marshall Railroad was chartered.

The first underground sewer was built.

The first Negro Church was organized by the Baptists.

The Detroit Female Seminary was opened.

May. The City Theater was opened.

May 18. The Ladies Protestant orphan asylum was started.

June 11. The first number of the Detroit Daily Advertiser appeared. It absorbed the Daily Express in 1845 and became the Detroit Tribune in 1849.

June 13. Harriet Martineau arrived in Detroit.

July. Washington A. Bacon opened a select school for boys.

July 1. _The Michigan State Register_, a semi-monthly publication, was first issued. Its last known issue was November 13, 1837.

October 20. _The Detroit Evening Spectator and Literary Gazette_ was published. The last number appeared in the Spring of 1838.

1837 Julius P. B. MacCabe published the first City Directory.

January 26. Michigan was admitted as a state to the Union.

April. Henry Howard was elected Mayor.

April 26. The Detroit Anti-Slavery Society was organized.

June 12. _The Spy in Michigan_, a weekly Whig paper, was first issued.

June 17. _The Michigan Observer_ first appeared and was discontinued after the issue of June 22, 1839.

July. The first issue of _The Detroit Morning Post_ was published. It was consolidated with _The Craftsman of Michigan_ as _The Morning Post and Craftsman_ in January, 1839 and ceased publication in 1840.

July 8. Daniel Webster arrived in Detroit. He gave a speech on July 11.

1838 Theodore H. Eaton founded the Eaton Chemical Dyestuff Company.

The first iron water pipes were laid.

The Detroit branch of the University of Michigan was established.

The Detroit school system was organized under the state public school law.

April. Augustus A. Porter was elected Mayor.

May. _The Craftsman of Michigan_ first appeared.

1839 A colored school was organized although no funds were immediately provided. In 1840 the State Legislature passed a law permitting the establishment of separate schools. They continued until 1869.

February 18. The Detroit Boat Club was organized.

March 18. The Second Baptist Church, colored, was organized.

March 27. Governor Mason approved an Act providing a new charter for Detroit. It changed the time of the annual election to the first Monday in March beginning in 1840. The city was divided into four wards.

April 1. De Garmo Jones was elected Mayor.

1840 George Miller began tobacco manufacturing at Detroit.

January. The Fire Department was established as a tontine insurance organization by the State. The Supreme Court invalidated it.

March. Zina Pitcher was elected Mayor.

1841 Black Methodists established the African M. E. Church.

April 13. The State Legislature empowered the Common Council to regulate the construction of drains and sewers, the erection of buildings, to pass fire prevention ordinances and to perform other duties.

May 25. Miss E. J. Vail opened a school for young ladies.

1842 Miss A. S. Bagg opened a school for young women.

Charles H. Miller began express service in Detroit.

The Detroit and Pontiac Railroad built a new station.

February 17. The Legislature passed an act establishing a school system under a Board of Education.

March. Dr. Douglass Houghton was elected

Mayor.

March 15. Detroit's first Board of Education was organized.

May. The Detroit Times was first published and continued until November, 1842.

May 25. The Constitutional Democrat was first issued as a semi-weekly. It was a weekly after October 1, 1842 and became a daily in 1844. It merged with The American Citizen in 1845 and ceased publication in the Spring of 1847.

July 8. Former President Martin Van Buren visited the city.

July 23. The Western Catholic Register was started by Eugene T. Smith and lasted for a year.

December 19. The Detroit Daily Gazette was first issued and continued for about three years.

1843 The Michigan Farmer succeeded The Western Farmer.

The St. John's German Evangelical School was established.

February 20. Percival C. Millette and Patrick Higgins opened a classical and English School.

March. Zina Pitcher was elected Mayor.

September. The American Vineyard, a temperance and anti-Catholic publication, was first issued. It continued until March 19, 1848.

December 4. The first Detroit Lodge of the Odd Fellows was chartered.

1844 The Grand Circus Park area was drained, filled and raised, thus beginning park development in the city.

Mrs. Elizabeth D. Bryant, cousin of William Cullen Bryant, began a select school.

March. John R. Williams was elected Mayor.

Spring. Stephen Fowler and Mr. Cochrane opened a classical school.

September 21. The <u>Allgemeine Zeitung</u>, a German democratic weekly, was first issued. Its name was changed in 1845 to the <u>Michigan Staats Zeitung</u>, and to <u>The Michigan Tribune</u> in 1850. It was merged with <u>The Michigan Democrat</u> in 1854.

November 18. <u>The Evangelical Observer</u> was first published, and existed for about two years.

December 28. The First Congregational Church and Society was organized.

1845 The Christ Church Society (Protestant Episcopal) was formed.

Horse-drawn public hacks were introduced in Detroit.

June 2. The <u>Daily Express</u> was first issued as an evening paper. It was published for six months until November 29, 1849.

June 9. St. Vincent's Hospital, the first hospital in Detroit, was opened under the sponsorship of four Sisters of Charity.

The Wayne County Building was first occupied.

July 4. Hog Island was renamed Belle Isle.

July 7. <u>The Detroit Daily News</u> was first published.

1846 May 4. Michigan abolished capital punishment.

1847 The state capital was moved from Detroit to Lansing. The old Capitol building was converted to school use.

The first horse-drawn streetcars began running on a regular schedule.

March. James A. Vandyke was elected Mayor.

April 24. The first company of soldiers left Detroit for the Mexican War.

May 22. The first German Reformed Methodist

Church, St. Matthew's, was incorporated. The trustees were organized on November 18, 1845.

October 20. The Detroit Merchants' Exchange and Board of Trade was formed.

November 29. The first "speed" telegraph line went into operation between Detroit and Ypsilanti.

DETROIT STANDS AS A CITY

1848 The Biddle House Hotel was built.

A new Michigan Central Depot was constructed.

The first bathtub was installed.

The National Theater was opened. It was renamed the Metropolitan Theater in 1859 and later the Varieties.

Uriah Gregory opened the first school to provide commercial training for students.

March 1. The telegraph line was completed between Buffalo and Detroit.

Horace Greeley visited Detroit.

March. Frederick Buhl was elected Mayor.

March 14. The City of Detroit Gaslight Company was organized. It began to supply streetlights in 1851.

March 29. The Western Excelsior was first published in the interest of the Negro population.

June 29. The Cathedral of Saints Peter and Paul was completed and consecrated.

July-September. The third epidemic of cholera occurred.

September 25-27. The first Michigan State Fair was held in Detroit.

Fall. The Peninsula Freeman, a free soil paper, was first issued.

1849 The Biddle House, a hotel, was opened.

Ulysses S. Grant was stationed at Detroit. He went to California in 1852.

The Wayne County Medical Society was established.

February 21. The second Presbyterian Church Society was organized.

March. Charles Howard was elected Mayor.

March 5. The Detroit Savings Fund Institute was founded, and articles of incorporation filed.

May 1. The Lafayette Street Methodist Church was formed.

July. Wellman's Literary Miscellany was first issued. Its name was changed to The Monthly Literary Miscellany in February, 1851.

September. Vice President Millard Fillmore visited the city.

November 19. The Detroit Daily Tribune was first issued. It merged with the Detroit News in 1915.

November 26. The Detroit Daily Herald was first published, continuing until December 6, 1850.

1850 The population of Detroit was 21,019.

A school for girls was established in the parish of St. Mary's. A school for boys was opened September 24, 1852.

The first passenger and freight service to be established between Detroit and Cincinnati was begun.

The Detroit Musical Association was formed.

W. D. Cochrane established the Detroit Business University.

January. The Monthly Hesperian and Odd Fellows' Literary Magazine was first issued. Its title was changed to The Monthly Hesperian and American Literary Magazine.

March. John Ladue was elected Mayor.

April 2. The Police Court was established.

Fall. The Western Evangelist, a weekly, was first published, and lasted for two years.

October 6. The First Congregational Unitarian Society was organized.

1851 March. Zachariah Chandler was elected Mayor.

April 21. The first Jewish Reformed Congregation was incorporated as Temple Beth El.

May. The Northwestern Musical Herald appeared.

May 17. The Peninsular Fountain, a temperance publication, was first issued. It continued for one year.

June. The first convent of the Religious of the Sacred Heart was opened.

June 5. The Sisters of Charity opened St. Vincent's Catholic Female Orphan Asylum.

September 24. The streets were lighted with gas for the first time by the Detroit Gaslight Company.

1852 Operation of the water supply was turned over to five trustees, and in 1853, the Board of Water Commissioners was created.

Railroads to Chicago and Toledo, Ohio were completed.

Zion German Reformed Lutheran School was organized.

March. John H. Harmon was elected Mayor.

May 12. The Michigan Organ of Temperance was started, and was consolidated with The Michigan Temperance Advocate in 1853.

September 27. The first Young Men's Christian Association was organized. It lasted until 1855.

Fall. The Free Democrat was established.

December. The Michigan Temperance Advocate was first published.

1853 The Board of Water Commissioners was created.

George B. Russell organized a company to manufacture railway cars. It was incorporated as the Detroit Car and Manufacturing Company in 1868.

April 30. The Detroit Catholic Vindicator was established. It merged with the Detroit Guardian in January, 1860.

May 1. The Michigan Volksblatt was first published. It was consolidated with the Democrat and renamed The Michigan Democrat and Volksblatt. Then it merged with the Michigan Staats Zeitung, and finally ceased publication in 1915.

October. The Michigan Homeopathic Journal appeared and lasted one year.

October 13. Amelia Bloomer lectured on women's rights.

1854 January. The Michigan Journal of Education and Teachers' Magazine was established and lasted until 1860.

January 18. The Daily Enquirer first appeared.

March. Oliver M. Hyde was elected Mayor.

May 30. A conference was held at Detroit which helped in organizing the Republican Party.

June-August. The fourth cholera epidemic occurred.

September. The Ashlar, a monthly, was first printed.

Fall. Miss C. E. Chapin opened a school.

1855 The Detroit Light Guard was organized. It

merged into the Michigan National Guard in 1911.

The State Legislature passed an act permitting the establishment of street railways in Detroit.

February 5. The Free Democrat and The Daily Enquirer were consolidated under the title of The Democrat and Enquirer.

March. Henry Ledyard was elected Mayor.

1856 Frederick Stearns began manufacturing drug specialities as a sideline to his drugstore. Frederick Stearns and Company was incorporated in 1882.

D. M. Richardson began to manufacture matches. He sold his firm to the Diamond Match Company in 1881.

A German and English School was established.

The railway connection between Detroit and Toledo was completed.

March. Oliver M. Hyde was elected Mayor.

March 1. The Medical Independent was begun. It became The Peninsular and Independent in March, 1857, and the last number was issued in March, 1860.

April. Misses Hosmer and Emerson opened a school.

May. The American Medical Association held its annual meeting in the city.

June 5. The Detroit Board of Trade was organized.

September. The Firemen's Journal was first issued.

December 4. Preston's United States Bank Note Reporter first appeared. It was published semi-monthly for about five years and then monthly until December, 1865.

1857 Brown's Reporter was first published by John Brown. It ceased publication in 1859.

January. <u>The Magazine of Travel</u> appeared and continued until 1858.

January 24. The Second Congregational or Free Church was organized.

February 5. An Act of the Legislature was approved by Governor Bingham which changed the name of the city to "The City of Detroit." Elections were to be held the first Monday in November. Officials were to take office the following January.

June 2. Sixty ladies organized The Industrial School to end begging by children who went up to houses. The School was started October 5, 1857.

July 16. The first telegraph cable was laid across the Detroit River.

September 24. The Russell House was opened and replaced the National Hotel.

November 3. Oliver M. Hyde was elected Mayor.

November 30. The Marine Hospital opened.

1858 The Berry Brothers established the first varnish factory.

The railroad from Detroit to Port Huron completed the connection with the Grand Trunk System.

January 12. The Recorder's Court was established to replace the Mayor's Court.

November. John Patton was elected Mayor.

1859 The merchants combined to pay for a police patrol of the business districts.

February 4. William Harper gave a gift of 1,000 acres for establishment of the Harper Hospital which was incorporated May 4, 1863. It first served as a center for treatment of sick and wounded soldiers, and was opened for civilian patients in January, 1866.

March 12. John Brown arrived in Detroit with fourteen slaves from Missouri. He met with leaders of the insurrectionary movement after a lecture by Frederick Douglass, and arranged for a raid on the South, which broke out prematurely at Harper's Ferry.

April 12. The first national championship billiard match was held in Detroit. Michael Phelan defeated John Serreiter.

September. The Detroit Female Seminary was founded.

The Young Men's Journal and Advocate of Temperance was first published, and continued for two years when it was succeeded by another temperance paper, The Transcript.

1860 The city contracted for its first steam fire engine, and named it Lafayette No. 1. Paid fire companies were organized.

Sister Mary DeSales established a home for the insane, which developed into St. Joseph's Retreat.

January 30. The first post office building was opened. It was also used for courts.

March 17. The Spirit of the Week, a military and sporting paper, was first issued.

May. The Home for the Friendless was begun by the Ladies' Christian Union.

July 10. General Lewis Cass gave the land for Cass Park to the city.

September 1. Philo M. Patterson's school for boys was organized.

September 4. William H. Seward spoke at a Republican meeting.

September 20. The Prince of Wales, later King Edward VII, came to Detroit.

September 28. Dorothea Dix inspected the Wayne County Poor House and Asylum finding the conditions there deplorable.

October 15. Stephen A. Douglas spoke at a Democratic meeting.

November. Christopher H. Buhl was elected Mayor.

December. <u>The People's Press</u> first appeared, continuing until April, 1861.

1816 Jeremiah and James Dwyer began the manufacture of stoves.

The Detroit House of Correction was opened.

March 12. An act was passed establishing a regular police force, with a police commission consisting of the Mayor and two appointed members.

May 2. The First Michigan Infantry was sworn in, leaving for service in the Civil War on May 13.

May 15. Governor Blair approved an act of the Legislature which appropriated 25,000 acres of state swamp land for the creation of German-American Seminary. It was not successful as a teachers' training institute. Then, it was made into a German school for boys and girls.

September 27. Sharrey Zadek Jewish Society was organized as the first Orthodox Synagogue in Detroit.

1862 July. The 24th Michigan Infantry was recruited to serve the Union in the Civil War. Its members came from Detroit and Wayne County.

July 8. The <u>Detroit Daily Advertiser</u> and the <u>Detroit Daily Tribune</u> were merged.

November. William C. Duncan was elected Mayor.

C. S. Bushnell, John A. Griswold, Eben N. Wilcox and Nehemiah D. Spery were granted the right to build and operate a Street Railway system.

1863 The Detroit Bridge and Iron Works was established.

H. G. Jones began a boys' school.

The Second National Bank was established. It took over the American Exchange National Bank in 1912. Its new name in 1914 was the First and Old Detroit National Bank.

An anti-Negro riot occurred. This led to a broad piece of legislation which gave great regulatory powers to a board of four commissioners.

March 19. Governor Blair approved an act of the Legislature incorporating the Detroit Board of Trade and Chamber of Commerce.

May 4. Harper Hospital was incorporated. It first served as a military hospital.

May 18. The school board decided to establish a district library from city fines.

June 21. The Articles of Association of the First National Bank were signed in accordance with the National Bank Act in 1862. The bank was opened October 5.

July 18. Frederick S. Porter began publication of <u>The Detroit Free Union</u>.

August 3. The first horse cars were run on Jefferson Avenue.

Fall. <u>The True Democrat</u> was published as a campaign paper.

1864 The Salem Lutheran School was started.

January. The American Homeopathic Observer, a monthly, was established, and continued until December, 1885.

July 18. St. Luke's Hospital and Church Home was opened.

September 27. The first draft was held to fill the Detroit quota for the Union Army. The second draft was conducted on March 21, 1865.

October. Free mail delivery by carriers was begun in Detroit.

October 2. The Daily Sun was first published.

November. Kirkland C. Barker was elected Mayor.

December 12. Froth, an illustrated comic weekly, first appeared. It ceased publication in November, 1865.

1865 The Michigan Car Company Works was established.

The Metropolitan Police Department was organized under state authority. The Police Commission first met on March 9.

The Detroit Journal of Commerce, a weekly, was established. It merged with The Daily Sun in 1871 and continued until 1876.

March 25. The School District Library was opened to the public in the rear of the old Capitol Building.

July 11-14. A Commercial Convention was held in the city.

August 12. General Ulysses S. Grant visited Detroit.

DETROIT AFTER THE CIVIL WAR

1866 The Spencerian Business College, founded at Albion, Michigan in 1860, moved to Detroit. It was consolidated with the Detroit Business University in 1885.

An experimental fire alarm telegraph system was installed, but it did not work well.

Hazen S. Pingree and Charles H. Smith established a boot and shoe factory.

Immanuel Evangelical Lutheran School was formed.

January. Harper Hospital was opened for civilian patients.

February 6. General William Tecumseh Sherman visited the city.

March 27. The Detroit Daily Post began publication. The Post and Tribune, which was first issued on October 14, 1877, eventually merged with the former. The title was changed to The Daily Post, August 1, 1884.

April. The Detroit Review of Medicine and Pharmacy was established. It later merged with the Peninsular Journal of Medicine.

May 31. The Wayne County Medical Society, second of that name, was formed and existed until 1876.

July 1. The Familien Blaetter, a German republican weekly, was first published.

September 4. President Andrew Johnson visited Detroit.

October 26. Dr. Samuel P. Duffield and Harvey C. Parke organized Duffield, Parke and Company. George S. Davis joined the firm in 1867, and it became known as Parke, Davis and Company in 1871.

November. Merrill I. Mills was elected Mayor.

1867 D. M. Ferry and Company, seed producers, was established.

January 1. Car ferry service across the Detroit River was begun on the Great Western by the Great Western Railway.

March 26. The Board of Fire Commissioners was created.

May 26. St. Anthony's Male Orphan Asylum was opened.

September 23. The Mechanic and Inventor was first issued. It merged with The Scientific Manufacturer in December, 1874 and was called The Scientific Manufacturer and Patent Intelligencer.

1868 The Detroit and Cleveland Navigation Company was incorporated.

The Detroit College of Medicine and Surgery was established.

William Davis of Detroit obtained a patent for a refrigerator railway car.

The Grand River Avenue Street Railway was begun.

April. The Detroit and Cleveland Steam Navigation Company was incorporated.

September 5. The Detroit Abend-Post, an evening paper, was established.

October 17. Baptist Tidings, a monthly was first issued.

November. William M. Wheaton was elected Mayor.

1869 An act was passed permitting the establishment of Savings Institutions.

Providence Hospital was founded for small children.

Grace Hospital was established.

The city installed the Gamewell Fire Alarm System.

The House of Providence for destitute children and unfortunate women was organized.

January 1. The Agricultural and Horticultural Journal was first published, and continued until 1887.

February 2. The first session of the Detroit College of Medicine was held at Harper Hospital.

March 29. The Detroit Opera House was Opened.

May 15. A new weekly paper The Michigan Farmer and State Journal of Agriculture was first issued.

June 5. The Women's Hospital and Foundlings' Home was incorporated. It had been organized in 1868 and was renamed the Woman's Hospital in 1927.

October 11. Colored children were first admitted to the public schools

1871 The population of Detroit was 79,577.

The Mutual Gaslight Company was established.

George M. Pullman bought the Detroit Car and Manufacturing Company. Detroit was the center for Pullman Car manufacturing until the plant near Chicago was erected.

Patrol wagon service was introduced by the police department.

January 1. <u>The Song Journal</u> was first published. It ceased publication in April, 1877.

January 2. The People's State Bank was begun.

January 19. <u>L'Êtoile Canadienne</u> was first issued and continued for a year.

April 15. Governor Baldwin approved an act of the Legislature providing for appointment of a board of park commissioners, and the purchase of land for a public park.

April 28. A meeting organized the Wayne County Savings Bank.

May. A new City Hall was occupied two months ahead of the July 1 deadline.

September 12. The Detroit, Lansing and Northern Railroad was opened from Detroit to Greenville.

October 9. A citizens' meeting raised $25,000 for the victims of the Chicago fire.

December 13. The first national waterway convention met in Detroit to improve access to the seaboard.

1872 The Mutual Gas Company was organized.

The Moffat Building with the first passenger elevator in the city was opened.

January. <u>Our Yankee Land</u>, a monthly, was first published. It continued until October, 1873.

The Trust Security and Safe Deposit Company of Detroit was organized.

The Trust Security and Safe Deposit Company of Detroit was organized.

Spring. The last annual town meeting was held. It had met since 1802.

September 28. The Western Home Journal, a Catholic weekly, was first issued. It became known as The Michigan Catholic in 1885.

November. Hugh Moffat was elected Mayor.

1873 St. Paul's Second German Evangelical School was established.

The Board of Public Works was established.

The Detroit and Bay City Railroad was completed to Bay City.

All stage coach lines from Detroit stopped operating.

The Congress and Barker Street Railway Lines began operating.

March 28. The State Legislature passed an act creating the Board of Estimates.

August 23. The Evening News, predecessor of the Detroit News was first issued by James Edmund Scripps. In 1891 Mr. Scripps purchased the Detroit Tribune and eventually consolidated it with the News. On November 30, 1884, the News brought out a Sunday edition. It was amalgamated with the Sunday Tribune on October 15, 1893, and entitled The Sunday News-Tribune.

September. The Scientific Manufacturer first appeared.

October 1. The Michigan Christian Advocate was organized as The Adrian District Methodist. In December the paper was enlarged and the former name adopted. In September, 1874, the Detroit Conference adopted it as its official publication, and it was moved to Detroit. It was finally issued as a weekly on January 1, 1875.

November. Our Diocese, a Protestant paper was established. It merged with The Living

Church of Chicago in February, 1880.

1874 The Detroit Conservatory of Music was established.

Mrs. David Thompson contributed $10,000 for the establishment of the Thompson House for Old Ladies.

March 27. A meeting was held to organize the Detroit Scientific Association at the hall of Professor J. M. B. Sill. Its constitution was adopted April 10. The Museum opened in May.

May 19. The Public Leader, devoted to the interests of the wine, beer, and liquor merchants, was begun.

June 2. The American Medical Association held its 25th meeting in Detroit.

1875 Evening schools were first maintained for children unable to attend during the day.

The Central Market, Cass Avenue and Third Street Railway Lines were opened.

January 1. Truth for the People, a momthly. was begun. Its name was changed to The Michigan Truth Teller, and it was finally discontinued in 1880.

May 3. An act of the Legislature was passed adding territory from Greenfield, Hamtramck and Springwells townships to Detroit.

September 13. C. J. Whitney's Opera House opened.

December. The Detroit Weekly Price Current was first issued. It ceased publication in November, 1882.

1876 N. Schrantz established a German and English academy.

The Detroit Courier, formerly the Wayne County Courier, established May, 1870, was moved to Detroit.

The Russel Wheel and Foundry Company was begun and incorporated in January, 1883.

The Company turned out the first car wheels in the West.

Rev. A. B. Brown opened a Boys' School.

August. A third Wayne County Medical Society was incorporated.

October 12. Le Courier, a literary weekly was begun. The title was soon changed to Le Journal de Detroit. It ceased publication in 1877.

November. Alexander Lewis was elected Mayor.

1877 The first telephone lines were installed in Detroit.

The Advertiser and Tribune was consolidated with The Detroit Daily Post.

The United States Savings Bank was founded.

January. The Medical Advance was established by Dr. C. H. Leonard and was published for three years, when it was succeeded by Leonard's Illustrated Medical Journal in 1880.

January 22. The Public Library building was formally dedicated.

February 9. Henry Ward Beecher delivered an address at the Detroit Opera House.

February 17. The Michigan Savings Bank was organized and opened on April 2, 1877.

March 6. M. C. Kellogg made the first telephone exhibition in the rooms of the Detroit Club.

March 17. The Detroit Daily Hotel Reporter and Railway Guide was first issued.

May. Emil Schober established The Michigan Railway Guide, a monthly.

July. The Fathers of the Society of Jesus announced that they were going to open Detroit College. It was officially opened in September. On January 10, 1911 the name was changed to the University of Detroit.

August 15. W. A. Jackson installed the first telephone in Detroit.

October 13. The Socialist, a weekly, owned by the Detroit section of the Socialist Labor Party was first issued. It merged with The National Socialist of Cincinnati in June, 1878.

October 14. The Detroit Post and Tribune was first issued. It was a consolidation of the Detroit Daily Tribune and the Detroit Daily Post.

1878 The first telephone exchange was opened.

The Detroit Athletic Club was organized.

The Merchants' and Manufacturers' Exchange was established.

The Detroit Association of Charities was organized.

January. The Michigan Medical News was first issued. It became the Medical Age in January, 1883.

February 28. The Detroit National, a greenback party organ, was first issued and continued for a year. Then it merged with Every Saturday.

June 16. The first phonograph was exhibited in Detroit.

August 15. Telephone service was begun.

September. The Detroit Home and Day School was opened.

November. George C. Langdon was elected Mayor.

November 14. The Michigan Homestead first appeared. It merged with The Agricultural World of Grand Rapids in September, 1880.

1879 St. Peter's German Evangelical School was established.

Detroit Every Saturday, a social, sporting and dramatic weekly journal, was established and continued for about eight years.

The State Legislature passed a bill authorizing construction of Grand Boulevard. It was formally dedicated in 1883.

April 8. The city purchased Belle Isle for a public park.

April 27. A "Tent" of the Knights of the Maccabees was established.

May. The Universalist Church was organized.

May 31. The Popular Era, a paper for colored people, first appeared. It was discontinued in November.

June. The Michigan College of Medicine was organized and opened November 17. It eventually closed.

July 12. Public Spirit, an illustrated weekly, was issued until October 4, 1879. It then became The Detroit Graphic and was discontinued in February, 1881.

September 18. President Rutherford B. Hayes visited Detroit.

October. Moore's Masonic Messenger, a monthly, was first published. It was discontinued in March, 1881 when Mr. Moore died.

November. William G. Thompson was elected Mayor.

November 9. The Sunday Herald was first issued. In June, 1881, the owner bought The Detroit Times. The Herald was discontinued November 20, 1881.

November 17. The Michigan College of Medicine opened.

1880 A music hall was converted into White's Grand Theater. It burned down in the fire of January, 1886.

The Detroit Council of Trades and Labor Unions was formed. It was reorganized in 1906 as the Detroit Federation of Labor.

The Brush Light Electric Light Company was organized.

January. The Northwestern Review, a literary monthly, was first issued and continued until 1882.

The Labor Review, a monthly, was established continuing until July. It was revived in August, 1881, and finally ceased publication in March, 1882.

April 15. The Detroit Copper and Brass Rolling Mills was incorporated.

April 22. The Detroit Association of Charities was formally established.

November. William Thompson was reelected Mayor.

November 29. The Detroit Baseball Club was organized. It was a member of the National League from 1881 to 1888. It played its first game in 1881.

1881 James Dwyer formed the Peninsular Stove Company.

Administration of the Public Library was turned over to the Library Commission by the Board of Education.

A Normal Training School to prepare teachers for the public schools was established. It became the Detroit Teachers College in 1921 and was later renamed the Wayne University School of Education.

January. The Microscope, a monthly, was first issued at Ann Arbor. It moved to Detroit in 1887 and continued until about 1893.

March 8-9. Sarah Bernhardt appeared at Whitney's Opera House.

March 26. Chaff, a society paper. was first issued. It ceased publication on November 15, 1885.

April 12. The State Legislature passed an act abolishing the board of estimates, conferring all powers of that body upon a board of councilmen of twelve members elected at large.

May 4. The Detroit Bar Association was organized.

May 26. The first provision was made for the Board of Health.

August 14. The Wabash Railroad entered Detroit.

August 29. The Council changed the name of Belle Isle to Belle Isle Park.

1882 The Detroit Steam Radiator Company was organized by Henry C. and Charles C. Hodges. It was the first to manufacture cast-iron radiators which became standard the world over.

A boys' school was established at St. Pauls' Protestant Episcopal Church.

The Board of Park Commissioners arranged for the Detroit Opera House Orchestra to give weekly band concerts at Belle Isle.

A franchise was granted to the Brush Electric Company to construct lines in the street. It did not begin street lighting until later because of the opposition of the gas companies.

May. The Indicator, a semi-monthly journal, devoted to insurance topics, was issued.

August 8. The Evening Telegraph, a daily, was first issued and continued until October 23, 1882. It was then published as The Detroit Daily Times from October 26, 1882 to January 31, 1883.

December 6. A meeting was held at James F. Joy's home to organize the Art Loan Exhibition of 1883. This was the beginning of the Detroit Museum of Art.

1883 The first electric arc lighting in Detroit was placed on Jefferson and Woodward.

January 27. Incandescent lights were first used in Metcalf's dry goods store.

April. The National People, an organ for colored people, was first issued and was finally discontinued in July, 1883.

April 5. United States Senator Thomas W. Palmer gave $10,000 in securities to William A. Moore for the city to aid in purchasing a lot and erecting an art gallery. The museum was opened to the public on September 1, 1888.

May 16. The Detroit Plain Dealer, a weekly for the colored population, was first published, continuing until 1895.

June 5. The State Legislature passed an act with many amendments to Detroit's Charter so that it became practically a new organic law.

August 24. The Art Loan Building was completed.

September 1. The Detroit Evening Journal was first published.

September 5. The Detroit Zoological Garden was established.

December 4. The Detroit Times, a morning paper, first appeared. It was suspended with the issue of February 26, 1885.

1884 The Sonntags Herold was first issued and continued until 1911.

The Kinder Post, a Sunday morning paper, was started and continued until 1912.

May. The American Meteorological Journal was established and continued until 1887.

May 1. The Dime Savings Bank was opened.

May 20. The Detroit Trade Journal was first issued and was later known as the Detroit Trade Journal and Michigan Courier. It lasted for ten years.

August 28. The Center, a weekly temperance journal, successor to The Michigan Prohibitionist, was first published. Its name was changed to The Center on April 25, 1885.

The paper was published until the early 1890's.

November. S. B. Grummond was elected Mayor.

November 1. The Labor Leaf was first issued by the Detroit Typographical Union as a campaign paper. Its title was changed to The Advance and Labor Leaf on February 19, 1887.

November 15. The Freemason, a weekly paper, was first published and survived until the early 1890's.

1885 The following papers were first published: The Michigan Builder, a weekly, which lasted until 1888, and The River Gazette, a weekly, continuing until 1887.

The following journals were begun: The Song Journal. which was succeeded by The Concert Goer in 1895 and finally ceased publication in 1905; The Central Mirror, a weekly publication of the Central Methodist Church which continued for about ten years; The Health Record; and The Visitor's Gazette which continued until 1900.
The Detroit Museum of Art was incorporated.

January. The Michigan Club was organized to study the civil and political institutions of the state and nation.

June. The Detroit College of Medicine was incorporated by the merger of the Detroit Medical College and the Michigan College of Medicine.

June 6. Buffalo Bill Cody and his Wild West Company appeared in Detroit with Sitting Bull as the star.

1886 Belle Isle Zoo was first begun as a deer park.

The following journals were established: Der Menschenfreund and The International Masonic Review which continued until the early 1890's.

Electric streetcars of the Highland Park Railway began operation on Woodward Avenue.

April 15. The Edison Illuminating Company was organized. It began to deliver current in November, 1886.

November. M. H. Chamberlain was elected Mayor.

December 6. Grance Hospital, founded in 1886 with donations from John McMillan and John S. Newberry, was opened.

1887 The following publications were issued: The Detroit Dash, issued by the Western Newspaper Union in the interest of the newspaper fraternity and was published for about ten years; The Bulletin of Pharmacy, and The Detroit Daily Hotel Reporter.

Mrs. Myrna B. Thomas founded the Thomas Normal Training School to train teachers in domestic science, physical and manual training.

April 17. Hotel Cadillac was opened.

April 19. The Central Savings Bank was organized.

May. The Arbeiter Zeitung was started and continued until July 14, 1889, and then the title was changed to the Michigan Arbeiter Zeitung.

November. John Pridgeon, Jr., was elected Mayor.

1889 The Detroit International Fair and Exposition was incorporated.

The ten-story Hammond Building was constructed. It was one of the first skyscrapers in the United States.

The following publications were first issued: Patriotic American, which lasted for a few years; The Church Messenger and Michigan Citizen, which continued for three years; The Detroit Churchman which was published until 1912; Gwiozda Detroicka, a weekly until 1893; The American Legal News; The Detroit Visitor and Michigan Hotel Reporter, continuing until 1893.

January 2. The Home Savings Bank was opened.

May 12. The first bridge to Belle Isle was constructed. It was burned down on April 27, 1915.

November. Hazen S. Pingree was elected Mayor. He began a regime of reform which greatly improved the administration of the city, including a reform of the utilities.

1890 The population of Detroit was 205,876.

The following publications were issued: The Collector, later called The Collector and Commercial Lawyer which lasted until 1905; Niedziela, a Polish illustrated weekly, which was discontinued in 1910; Once a Week, continuing for about eight years; Rope and Rubber, lasting for about four years; and The Saturday Night, continuing until 1897.

Midland Chemical Company, the predecessor of Dow Chemical Company, was organized.

The Boys' Home and D'Arcambal Association was developed.

May. The Building, Savings and Loan Review was first published and continued for four years.

December. The National Convention of the American Federation of Labor met at Detroit with Samuel Gompers presiding. Mary Burke was the first woman delegate to attend a national convention.

December 17. Thomas McGregor established the McGregor Institute, a charitable organization.

1891 The Y. M. C. A. established vocational educational classes which eventually grew into the Detroit Institute of Technology, chartered November 10, 1909.

April 21. The Street Car employees struck for a ten-hour day against the Detroit City Railway. A settlement was reached May 12.

October. The Union Trust Company was opened under the General Banking Act of 1891.

December 20. The Detroit College of Law opened.

1892 Henry Ford produced his first car.

Charles B. King of Detroit applied for a patent for his new invention, a pneumatic hammer. It was granted in 1894.

An act of the Legislature was passed placing the appointment of police commissioners in the hands of the Mayor. Mayor Pingree appointed four police commissioners July 13.

<u>The Retail Druggist</u>, a monthly pharmaceutical magazine, was established.

January 5. The Chamber of Commerce was organized at Philharmonic Hall.

January 12. Paderewski performed at the Detroit Opera House.

1893 The following publications were first issued: <u>The Law Students' Helper</u>; the <u>West Detroit Times</u>, a weekly newspaper; <u>The Bayview Magazine</u>; <u>The American Catholic Tribune</u>; and <u>The Plymouth Weekly and Christian Sociologist</u>.

Long-distance telephone service was inaugurated from Detroit to New York and Chicago.

The Detroit Gas Company was organized through the merger of the Detroit and Mutual Gaslight Companies.

Former United States Senator Thomas W. Palmer presented Palmer Park to the city.

The legislature passed an act providing for appointment of a board of six lighting commissioners.

The Detroit Bureau of Police appointed Mrs. Marie Owen the first policewoman in the United States.

March 16. The Detroit Young Women's Christian Association was founded.

April. The voters approved Mayor Pingree's proposal for municipal lighting.

November 7. Hazen S. Pingree was elected Mayor for a third time.

1894 Charles B. King drove the first gasoline car in Detroit.

The following publications were first issued: The Gleaner, whose title was changed to The Gleaner Forum in 1920; Trade, an independent weekly for the merchants of Michigan, Ohio and northern Indiana; and The Michigan Presbyterian.

The Detroit Yacht Club was founded.

September. The American Electrical Heater Company was incorporated.

DETROIT AND THE AGE OF THE AUTOMOBILE

1895 The following publications were established: The Leucocyte, a quarterly medical journal; The Detroit Legal News, a daily; The Stove Mounters' and Range Workers' Journal, monthly; The Motormen and Conductor, monthly official journal of the Amalgamated Association of the Street and Electric Railway Employees of America; and Justice, a weekly devoted to the single tax question.

The Detroit Federation of Women's Clubs was founded.

Kindergartens were opened in the public schools.

March 1. The City Board of Health was organized.

April 1. The municipal power station began to supply power for the street lighting system, and public buildings.

1896 The last horse car was operated on the Detroit streets. All electric streetcars were used thereafter.

February. The White Star Line was organized and incorporated.

June 4. Henry Ford drove his first automobile in Detroit.

1897 The Olds Company was organized by Ransom E. Olds and Frank Clark. Their first automobile was finished in 1898, but it did not run very impressively. The Company was finally reorganized in Detroit in 1899.

Sebastian S. Kresge opened a store in Detroit with J. G. McCory. Kresge took over full control in 1899. The main office of Kresge Company remained in Detroit.

March 20. The Michigan Supreme Court ruled that Hazen S. Pingree could not hold both offices of Mayor of Detroit and Governor of Michigan, so he resigned the mayoral post.

May 5. William C. Maybury was elected Mayor and held office through 1904.

October 7. The Detroit Opera House was completely burned. It was rebuilt and finally reopened on September 12, 1898.

1898 The following publications were established: Polonia Rekard, the oldest Polish paper and The Detroit Law Journal.

William E. Metzger opened the first independent automobile dealership.

February 8. The Detroit Society for the Prevention of Cruelty to Children was organized.

February 14. The First Church of Christ Scientist was organized.

April 6. William Jennings Bryan delivered an address in Detroit.

April 19. The first Michigan troops left for Cuba at the outbreak of the Spanish-American War.

1899 The Chandler Act was passed beginning the Michigan State Board of Registration in Medicine.

The American Boy, a weekly juvenile magazine, was first published.

1900 The population of Detroit was 285,704.

All streetcar lines were united into one

corporation: the Detroit United Railway.

Home Study, a monthly bookkeeping magazine, was first issued and survived until 1911.

January. The Chauncey Hurlbut Branch Library was opened as a delivery station. It was established as a full branch in September, 1905.

March. The Detroit Republican was first published and lasted until 1906. It was aimed at the colored population of the city.

April 2. The Henry M. Utley Branch Library was opened in the Central High School and moved to 1515 Woodward Avenue in March, 1905. It moved to its own building at 8726 Woodward Avenue in May, 1913.

April 16. The George S. Hosmer Branch of the Library was opened in the Harris High School. It moved to a building erected for it at 3506 Central Avenue on January 7, 1911.

April 19. The first game was played by the Detroit Tigers which had become a member of the newly formed American League.

June 8. Admiral George Dewey visited the city.

September 29. The Detroit Golf Links were formally opened.

October 1. The Detroit Evening Times was established under the name of Today. It was purchased by William Randolph Hearst late in 1921.

October 25. The Herbert Bowen Branch of the Library was opened in the Western High School. It moved to a new building in December, 1912.

December 8. The articles of Incorporation for the Detroit Trust Company were approved by the state.

1901 The Henry Ford Automobile Company was formed. Ford soon dropped out.

The Cadillac Company was incorporated.

The following publications were first issued: the <u>Michigan Degree of Honor Herald</u>, which continued until 1911, and the <u>Odontoblast</u>, issued by the students' dental department of the Detroit College of Medicine, existing until 1912.

May 4. A legislative act was passed establishing the office of Commissioner of Parks and Boulevards in place of the Board of Commissioners of Parks and Boulevards. In addition it provided for a Commissioner of Public Works and of the Police Department.

July 24. The Bi-Centenary exercises were opened in Detroit with the unveiling of the "Cadillac Chair" on Cadillac Square.

November 27. The United States Savings Bank was incorporated.

1902 The following journals were first published: <u>The Headlight</u>, a monthly which continued until 1911 and <u>Dongo</u>, a Hungarian semi-monthly humorous magazine.

February 27. The first automobile show in Detroit was given in the Light Guard Armory.

May 3. Carrie Nation delivered an address in Detroit.

June. Henry M. Leland and his son Wilfrid met with others and organized the Cadillac Motor Company. It was orginially the Detroit Automobile Company and then merged with Leland and Faulconer Manufacturing Company in 1909. Finally in 1910 it became the Cadillac Division of General Motors.

September. <u>The Michigan Investor</u> was first issued.

September 21. President Theodore Roosevelt was in Detroit to address the Spanish-American War Veterans Convention.

1903 The Packard Motor Company moved to Detroit.

The Buick Company was organized in Flint, Michigan.

The following publications were established:

The Michigan Union Advocate, which lasted for ten years, and Dziennik Polski, an evening daily.

January 20. The Detroit Edison Company was incorporated.

May 5. Booker T. Washington spoke in Detroit about the race problem in the South.

June 16. The Ford Motor Company was incorporated.

June 16. Henry Ford asked John F. and Horace E. Dodge to manufacture engines, transmissions and steering gears in quantity.

June 30. The Detroit Board of Commerce was formally established.

September 1. The Detroit Commercial College was opened by E. B. Winter.

December. The Packard Company began operations in Detroit after moving there from Warren, Ohio.

1904 A city ordinance was passed requiring the licensing of automobiles. It was upheld by the State Supreme Court on April 22, 1905.

The Maxwell-Briscoe Company was organized to produce the Maxwell Car. It eventually became the Maxwell Motor Company and was then purchased by Walter Chrysler in 1919 and later absorbed into the Chrysler Corporation.

Ransom Olds resigned from the Olds Company.

The following journals were first published: The Michigan Banker, Friendly Elk, and Concrete.

January. The Bulletin of the Institute of Art of the City of Detroit was established.

March 1. The John S. Gray Branch Library was opened. It moved to its new building at 1117 Field Avenue on June 1, 1906.

September 3. The Detroit Steel Products Company was incorporated to make automobile springs and "Harvey" friction gears.

November. George P. Codd was elected Mayor.

1905 The Detroit Business University was incorporated.

John A. Kunsky and A. Arthur Caille opened the first movie theater in Detroit called the "Casino."

The following publications were begun: Civic News, Detroit Realty Journal, Electrocraft, Gas Engine Age, Motor Talk, the Detroit American, and The Polish Daily, which ceased publication in 1910.

January. The Burroughs Adding Machine Comoany, organized in Detroit by William S. Burroughs was incorporated. It succeeded the American Arithmometer Company, organized in January, 1886 in St. Louis.

May 1. The city adopted standard time.

August 30. Ty Cobb began his baseball career with the Detroit Tigers.

1906 The Shrine Circus originated in Detroit.

The American State Bank of Detroit was organized.

A. F. Tull and L. C. Rauch founded the Business Institute of Detroit.

The Defense League of Detroit was formed as an integral part of the Wayne County Medical Society. The purpose was to defend any member of the society accused of malpractice.

The Provident Loan Society of Detroit was organized.

May 11. The American Loan and Trust Company was incorporated.

June 5. James E. Scripps willed $50,000 to the city in order to beautify it .

July. The Security Trust Company was organized.

September 4. William Jennings Bryan addressed 115,000 people.

1907 William C. Durant combined the Olds Company and the Buick Company.

Two weekly journals were founded: Capital, concerning finance, and the Michigan Contractor and Builder.

March 2. The Detroit Saturday Night, a weekly newspaper, came into existence.

June 1. The National Bank of Commerce was founded.

July. The Detroit Stock Exchange was formed as part of the reorganization of the Detroit Brokers Association.

August. The Detroit Tigers won the American League pennant.

September 1. The West Fort Street Branch Library was opened on West End Avenue. It moved to 3327 West Jefferson Avenue on January 1, 1910 and then to another building at 5825 West Fort Street in September, 1913.

November. William B. Thompson was elected Mayor.

1908 The Ford Motor Company began producing the Model T exclusively. It produced 15 million Model T cars by 1927.

The following publications were first issued: The Lyceum World; The Little Stick, weekly; The Club Woman, monthly publication of the Detroit Federation of Women's Clubs; The North Side News; and The Trestle Board, a Masonic monthly.

The Jefferson Avenue School of modern languages was established.

April. The City Council passed an ordinance providing for the regular collection of waste throughout the city.

July 22. The Fisher Body Company was incorporated, and changed its name to the Fisher Closed Body Company on December 22, 1910.

September 16. General Motors Company was incorporated. It was organized by William C. Durant around the Buick and Oldsmobile Companies. The Cadillac, Pontiac and Chevrolet Companies were added later.

The Detroit Tigers won the American League pennant.

October 1. The Edwin F. Conley Branch Library was opened. It was moved to a buildin constructed for that purpose in September, 1913 at 4600 Martin Street.

October 8. The first automobile taxicabs with automatic fare registers appeared in Detroit.

November 8. The Hupp Motor Company was incorporated.

1909 The Dexter School for Boys was established.

The Federal Savings Bank was opened.

The following publications were first issued: the Magyar Ujsag; Hungarian News, a weekly; Beach's Magazine of Business; Knight's Progress, a fraternal monthly; The Detroit Leader, a weekly paper for colored residents; the Tribuna Italiana D'America, a weekly; and The Social Moose, a monthly fraternal magazine.

February 20. The Hudson Motor Car Company was organized and incorporated.

March 20. The C. M. Hall Lamp Company was incorporated to manufacture motor, motorcycle and bicycle lamps and accessories for electric and acetylene equipment.

May. The Common Council created the City Plan and Improvement Commission.

Fall. The Detroit Tigers won the American League pennant.

November. Philip Breitmeyer was elected Mayor.

1910 The Michigan State Auto School was opened to train men for positions in the automobile and parts factories, for garage and repair work.

Special education classes were begun for children with various handicaps.

La Voce del Popolo, a weekly Italian paper, was first published.

February 10. The Federal Motor Truck Company was incorporated.

March 22. After several years of discussion and controversy the City Council voted to accept Andrew Carnegie's gift of $750,000 for a library and branches, with agreement that the city would provide the sites and $75,000 per year for maintenance.

June 20. The Detroit Industrial Exposition was opened.

September. The Bulletin of the Detroit Board of Commerce was published and continued until January, 1911, when its name was changed to The Detroiter.

October 28. The Detroit Rotary Club was formed.

1911 The Dispatch-Reporter, weekly, and The Presbyterian Examiner were first published.

January 10. The University of Detroit, formerly Detroit College, was chartered.

January 12. The Commerce Motor Car Company, manufacturers of light delivery trucks, was incorporated.

January 15. The Detroit Tuberculosis Sanatorium was dedicated.

February 14. The Studebaker Corporation was incorporated as a consolidation of the Studebaker Brothers Manufacturing Company and the Everitt-Metzger-Flanders Company.

March. The Juvenile Detention Home was opened.

May 1. Herman Kiefer Hospital for contagious diseases began to admit patients.

September 18. President William Howard Taft visited Detroit.

November. William B. Thompson was elected Mayor.

December 11. The Detroit Zoological Society was organized.

1912 The first class for the blind was formed by the Detroit public schools.

The Standard Motor Truck Company was incorporated.

The Bloomfield Hills Seminary was begun.

The following publications were first issued: Quill, quarterly journal of Sigma Delta Chi, the journalism honorary; The Pilot, published by the Locomotive Engineer and Conductors' Manual Protective Association; and Michigan Business Farming.

February 5. Sir Robert Baden-Powell, founder of the Boy Scouts in England, was welcomed to Detroit.

Fall. The Detroit Tigers won the American League Pennant.

December 21. The George V. N. Lathrop Branch Library was opened in a building erected for it.

1913 The new Michigan Central Railroad Station was opened.

Detroit Labor News, a weekly publication of the Detroit Federation of Labor, and Rekord-Codzienny, the Polish Daily Record, were first published.

The following Belgian publications first appeared: the Gazette van Detroit, weekly; the Detroitenaar, weekly; and the Belgian Press. In addition the Magyar Hirlap, a Hungarian daily, and Russian Life were first issued.

The first profit-sharing plan of the Ford Company was inaugurated. The company also initiated the assembly-line.

The Dodge Brothers decided to manufacture their own car, and built a million-dollar plant at Hamtramck.

February 10. The voters rejected a proposed Charter revision.

February 26. The first concert of the Detroit Symphony Orchestra took place at the Detroit Opera House.

March 16. Clarence Munroe Burton presented his collection of books, pamphlets, letters, maps and prints and his former residence to the City of Detroit. The collection was moved to quarters in the new library building in March, 1921.

Spring. The First National Bank and the Old Detroit National Bank were consolidated.

August 25. The Merchants National Bank was opened.

September. The George Osius Branch Library was opened in its own building at 8530 Gratiot Avenue.

November 3. Some amendments to the City Charter were passed at the general elections.

1915 The Grosse Point School for girls and boys was established.

Postgraduate highschool training was first offered by the Board of Education ay Central High School. It developed into a junior college authorized by state law in 1917, and finally became Wayne State University.

Roy A. Fruehauf and his son Harvey built a trailer with hard rubber tires and open slat sides which was the first modern truck trailer in Detroit.

The Northwestern State Bank was incorporated.

February 1. The Tribune merged with the Detroit News.

February 6. The Hotel Statler was opened.

April. D. B. U. Topics, the journal of the

Detroit Business University, was first issued.

April 27. The Belle Isle Bridge burned.

October 1. Henry Ford Hospital was opened, although it was not completed until after World War I.

October 12. Detroit's municipally operated hospital was opened.

November 23. The Saxon Motor Car Corporation was incorporated.

1916 The Bank of Detroit was founded.

The Commonwealth Bank opened. It merged with the Federal Savings Bank as the Commonwealth-Federal Savings Bank.

The first registered Girl Scout Troop in Michigan was formed in Detroit.

<u>Black and White</u>, a monthly, and <u>The D. A. C. News</u>, a monthly journal of the Detroit Athletic Club, were first published.

The Bernard Ginsberg Branch Library at 91 Brewster and the Divie B. Duffield Branch Library at 2507 West Grand Boulevard were opened.

The Guaranty Trust Company was established.

April 24. The Michigan State Bank of Detroit was incorporated.

July. President Woodrow Wilson came to Detroit.

August 26. A referendum was passed approving creation of a new Board of Estimates which consisted of the Mayor, City Clerk, City Treasurer, City Controller and Corporation Counsel.

October 13. The General Motors Corporation was incorporated.

October 25. The Henry Ford Trade School opened.

1917 The following publications were first issued: <u>Varsity News</u>, school paper of the University of Detroit; <u>Civic Searchlight</u>, by the Detroit Citizens' League; the <u>Detroit Banker</u>; the <u>News Letter</u>, by the Detroit Chapter of the American Red Cross; <u>Northern Navigator</u>; <u>The State</u>, by the YMCA; <u>The Tamarack</u>, by the University of Detroit; and the <u>American State Banker</u>.

The creation of the Children's Museum was sponsored by the Detroit Museum of Art and the Board of Education.

42 different agencies were brought together in a Community Union or Detroit Patriotic Fund. A single seven days' drive was arranged to raise the amount of money needed.

The Lincoln Motor Company was first incorporated for the Manufacture of Liberty Motors. Its principle organizers were Henry M. and Wilfrid C. Leland.

May 12. The Bankers Trust Company of Detroit was incorporated.

August. The Industrial Morris Plan Bank of Detroit was incorporated.

November 6. A proposition to revise the City Charter was passed.

December 2. The Detroit United Railway raised fares from three to five cents.

1918 The Detroit Museum of Arts became a city institution under a Municipal Arts Commission.

The Detroit branch of the Federal Reserve Bank was opened.

<u>The Social Secretary</u> was first published as an annual social and club directory.

April 24. Women were employed as mail carriers.

May. Chevrolet joined the General Motors Corporation.

June. Fort Shelby Hotel was opened.

June 25. The new Detroit City Charter was adopted by the voters. It provided for initiative and referendum, and that all elected officers were subject to recall.

July 1. The Detroit College of Medicine and Surgery was taken over by Detroit as a city-owned institution.

November 5. James Couzens was elected Mayor. He took office in January and held it until December 5, 1922, when he resigned to enter the United States Senate.

December. United Motors joined the General Motors Corporation.

1919 The Detroit Council of Churches was organized.

The Detroit Motorbus Company was incorporated.

General Motors acquired an important interest in the Fisher Body Corporation.

The following publications were first issued: Francais Pour Tous, literary and educational journal; Building Materials, a monthly; and the Jewish Way (Der Weg).

January. Real Estate, the official journal of the Detroit Real Estate Board, was published.

The Arts Commission came into being. It assumed operation and maintenance of the Detroit Museum of Art beginning July 1, 1919.

March 5. Detroit women voted for the first time in a general primary election.

April. The Michigan Architect and Engineer was established.

June. The Blue Triangle, a monthly publication of the Young Women's Christian Association, was first issued.

July. Twenty-five aliens were deported as part of the "Red" scare in Detroit, 1919-20.

August. The Women Lawyers Association of Michigan was organized with five members.

December 18. General Pershing visited Detroit.

1920 The population of Detroit was 993,678.

The Department of Recreation was established.

January. The <u>Detroit Masonic News</u> first appeared.

April 5. The voters agreed to have the city acquire, own, and operate the street railway system, and approved a bond issue for its financing.

August 17. The first air-mail delivery arrived from Cleveland.

May 23. The Pennsylvania Railroad initiated train service from Detroit.

August 20. WWJ began broadcasting of regular progress. It was the first commercial radio station in the United States licensed on October 13, 1921.

November 3. The Wayne County and Home Bank of Highland Park was established.

1921 The Continental Bank of Detroit was established.

Goodwill Industries began operating in Detroit.

The General Motors Building was completed.

February 2. The city began operation of a municipal street car system.

February 23. President-elect Warren G. Harding named Edwin Benby, Detroit lawyer, Secretary of the Navy in his Cabinet.

March. Detroit's Library Building was opene to the public.

May. <u>The Detroit Golfer</u> was first issued.

July 27. The Memorial Fountain was dedicat

in Grand Circus Park in honor of General Russell A. Alger.

August 1. The Commercial State Savings Bank opened for business.

September 29. The Detroit Mutual Savings and Loan Association was organized.

October 6. William R. Hearst purchased the Detroit Times.

1922 Regular airplane service was arranged between Detroit and Chicago and Cleveland, mainly for air mail.

The Detroit Historical Society was created.

The Merrill-Palmer Nursery School was opened.

Detroit was the first city to use a police broadcasting system with radio-equipped cars to receive messages.

January 4. Henry Ford purchased the Lincoln Motor Company for $8,000,000.

March 25. The Ford Motor Company adopted a 40-hour week.

April 10. Horsedrawn fire-fighting equipment was last used in Detroit. The Department was entirely motorized.

April 17. The voters approved the purchase by the Detroit United Railway of remaining lines and properties which were taken over on May 15 by the city.

May 4. Radio Station WJR received its license.

July 21. The Detroit News was absorbed by the Detroit Journal.

December 5. Mayor Couzens resigned to become a United States Senator. John C. Lodge became Acting Mayor.

December 8. Isadora Duncan gave a dance recital at the Orchestra Hall.

1923 April 2. Frank E. Doremus was elected Mayor.

September. The first traffic school for automobile drivers was held in the police auditorium.

September. The streetcar fare rose from five to six cents.

September 10. The four-year College of the City of Detroit opened.

November 1. The new Belle Isle Bridge was opened. It was renamed the Douglas MacArthur Bridge on February 25, 1942.

November 5. Mayor Frank E. Doremus was re-elected.

1924 The Detroit College of Music opened.

The first Chrysler car was produced.

October 14. The Prince of Wales, later Edward VIII, visited the city.

November. John W. Smith was elected Mayor. He served until 1927.

December 8. The Book-Cadillac Hotel was opened.

1925 Henry W. Reichhold established Reichhold Chemicals.

June 3. Radio Station WXYZ received its license.

June 6. The Chrysler Corporation was incorporated, absorbing the Maxwell Company and Chalmers.

June 14. The Bonstelle Theater was opened in the remodeled Temple Beth El. It closed on January 11, 1934.

October 8. Henry Ford produced his first airplane.

1926 February. The first contract airmail service from Detroit to Cleveland was begun and flown in a Ford plane.

March. The City Plan Commission adopted a zoning ordinance.

May 9. Richard E. Byrd used a Detroit-built plane, the Josephine Ford, in his flight over the North Pole.

May 19. Sebastian S. Kresge founded a $25,000,000 organization to provide for education, religion and charity.

September 5. The Cass Theater was opened.

September 25. The Detroit Cougars, formally the Victoria Cougars of Canada, entered the National Hockey League. They were renamed the Falcons and later the Red Wings.

November 3. Ty Cobb left the Detroit Tigers and retired from baseball.

1927 May 26. The last Model T Ford was produced. The Model A was shown in December.

August 10. Charles Lindbergh's birthplace at 1120 West Forest Avenue was dedicated with a plaque in honor of his transatlantic flight.

October 6. The Detroit Institute of Arts building was opened and dedicated on October 8.

October 15. The new Olympia Stadium was opened.

October 24. The Detroit City Airport was opened. It was dedicated November 5.

November 8. John C. Lodge was elected Mayor of Detroit and served until 1929.

1928 The Detroit Civic Theater was organized.

July 30. The Dodge Motor Company merged with the Chrysler Corporation.

August 1. The Detroit Zoological Park was opened.

1929 March 26. Detroit won a national fire prevention contest.

June 2. The Woman's Hospital was opened.

June 3. The Children's Village of the Methodist Children's Home was dedicated.

August 26. The Dirigible <u>Graf Zeppelin</u> arrived in the city on its world tour.

November 5. Charles W. Bowles was elected Mayor.

November 11. The Ambassador Bridge between Detroit and Windsor was dedicated. Traffic began to cross it on November 15.

1930 The Covered Wagon Company of Detroit initiated an important advance when it started manufacturing the "Covered Wagon" trailer coach or mobile home.

July 22. The first recall occurred in a major city, when Mayor Charles Bowles was recalled at a special election.

September 9. Frank Murphy was elected Mayor. He assumed office on September 23.

November 23. The Detroit-Windsor Vehicular Tunnel under the Detroit River was opened.

1931 January 2. An unemployment relief demonstration was held in front of city hall.

April 14. Henry Ford built his 20,000,000th automobile.

June 20. Fifty members of the Police Department were indicted for various crimes by a Grand Jury.

November 7. Mayor Murphy was reelected.

1932 January 5. Salaries of city employees and welfare expenditures were cut drastically because of the fiscal crisis.

October 2. Franklin D. Roosevelt, Democratic Presidential nominee, spoke at a political rally.

1933 March 29. 10,000 Detroiters met in the Naval Armory to protest German persecution of various minorities.

May 6. Frank Murphy resigned as Mayor because he was appointed Governor-General of the Philippines. Frank Couzens became Mayor on May 10.

November 27. Frank Couzens was elected Mayor.

1934 Henry Ford supervised renovation of Botsford Tavern which was opened to the public.

January. The City University was named Wayne University. It had been formed by the merger of various colleges of the City, the Medical, Teachers and Liberal Arts.

September 24. The Detroit Tigers won their first American League Pennant in twenty-five years.

October 9. The Detroit Tigers were defeated in the World Series by the St. Louis Cardinals, four games to three.

1935 September 21. The Detroit Tigers won the American League Pennant.

October 7. The Detroit Tigers won the World Series, defeating the Chicago Cubs four games to one.

November 7. Mayor Couzens was reelected,

The Detroit Lions defeated the New York Giants and won the Football League title.

1936 Natural gas was first piped from Texas to Detroit. Manufactured gas had been used previously.

January 20. Edsel Ford established the Ford Foundation.

April 11. The Detroit Red Wings won the National Hockey League playoffs and thus the Stanley Cup.

October 15. President Franklin D. Roosevelt visited Detroit.

1937 Detroit was established as an Archbishopric with Edward A. Mooney as its first Archbishop.

January 13. The Lone Ranger Program was first broadcast over radio station WXYZ.

February 11. General Motors recognized the United Auto Workers Union after a three-month strike.

April 6. The one-month strike against Chrysler was ended.

April 15. The Detroit Red Wings won the National Hockey League playoffs and the Stanley Cup.

May 3. William Knudsen became President of General Motors.

The United Brotherhood of America, or Black Legion, an anti-union subversive organization made its headquarters in Detroit.

May 26. A clash occurred between Ford Company guards and leaders of the United Auto Workers.

June. Joe Louis of Detroit won the world's heavyweight boxing championship.

November 2. Richard W. Reading was elected Mayor.

1938 April 11. The Church of the Blessed Sacrament was proclaimed the Cathedral of the Catholic Archdiocese of Detroit.

October. Tenants began living in the first units of the Brewster and Parkside housing projects.

November 20. Detroiters joined a nationwide prayer service protesting Nazi persecution of religious minorities, especially Jews.

1939 November 7. Edward J. Jeffries, Jr. was elected Mayor of Detroit. He took office on January 2, 1940 and served for six terms.

1940 April 3. John S. Knight purchased the Detroit Free Press.

April 6. The Ford Motor Company completed its construction of its 28,000,000th automobile.

August 15. The Chrysler Corporation started building a $20,000,000 plant to make large army tanks as part of the preparedness effort.

September 27. The Detroit Tigers clinched the American League Pennant.

October 8. The Tigers lost the World Series to the Cincinnati Reds, four games to three.

December 12. The Hudson Motor Company agreed to a contract for the first union shop in a major automobile plant with the United Auto Workers.

December 19. William S. Knudsen, President of General Motors Corporation, was named head of the United States National Defense Council.

1941 January 7. William S. Knudsen was named Director of the Office of Production Management.

April 14. The Ford Motor Company recognized the United Auto Workers and signed a contract after a ten-day strike.

May. Radio Station WWJ opened the first FM radio station in Michigan.

October 30. The Duke of Windsor visited war plants in Detroit.

December 8. Army guards were placed at the Detroit-Windsor Tunnel and Bridge after the Pearl Harbor attack by the Japanese on December 7.

1942 February 8. A clash between whites and Negroes occurred at the Sojourner Truth housing project.

May 4. The first United States ration book was issued in Detroit as part of the war effort.

July 2. Max Stephan of Detroit was found guilty of treason for aiding a Nazi prisoner of war to escape. He was the first American convicted of treason and sentenced to be executed since the Whiskey Rebellion in 1794.

President Roosevelt commuted the sentence to life imprisonment on July 1, 1943.

July 17-24. The Detroit Street Railway strike crippled city transportation.

September 18. President Roosevelt visited Detroit to examine the war plants.

November. The first occupants moved into the Herman Gardens Housing project. It was completed May, 1943.

1943 May 26. Edsel Ford died. He was 49 years old.

June 21. Negro-white race riots occurred. Federal troops were brought in to restore order.

September 27. The first Grand Opera Festival was held.

1944 January 11. The first season of the Civic Light Opera began.

January 13. Mayor Jeffries appointed an Inter-racial Relations Committee.

1945 Parke, Davis and Company introduced Promin, the first effective chemo-therapeutic agent for leprosy.

July. Reconversion to peacetime production began in the automobile plants.

July 13. Henry Reichhold purchased the Wilson Theater to provide a home for the Detroit Symphony Orchestra.

August 9. The Kaiser-Frazer Corporation was organized. Within two years it had become the fourth largest manufacturer of automobiles.

August 14. Detroit celebrated the surrender of Japan.

September 21. Henry Ford II was elected president of the Ford Motor Company upon the resignation of his grandfather.

September 30. The Detroit Tigers won the

American League Pennant.

October 10. The Tigers won the World Series, defeating the Chicago Cubs four games to three.

November 21. A strike was called against the General Motors Corporation. It lasted 113 days until March 14, 1946, when General Motors agreed to pay an 18 ½ cents per hour raise to the U.A.W.-C.I.O.

POST WORLD WAR II DETROIT -- URBAN RECONSTRUCTION

1946 Parke, Davis and Company introduced the anti-histaminic Benadryl.

January 1. Streetcar fares were raised to ten cents.

February 18. Archbishop Edward Mooney was made a Cardinal.

March 27. Walter Reuther was elected president of the United Auto Workers.

April 1. Workers struck against the Detroit Street Railway bringing transportation to a halt.

May 29. The Sesquicentennial of the raising of the American Flag over the area was celebrated.

June 9. The Automotive Golden Jubilee was celebrated.

1947 March 4. The City Council approved the City Plan Commission's riverfront development plan.

WWJ-TV began television broadcasting.

April 7. Henry Ford died. He was 83 years old.

May 29. Willow Run Airport was officially designated the airport for commercial airlines in the Detroit area.

July 9. A Smoke Abatement Code was adopted.

November 4. Eugene I. van Antwerp was elected Mayor.

1948 Parke, Davis and Company introduced the anti-biotic Chloromycetin.

The Ford Foundation became the largest in the world when it received the Ford Motor Company non-voting stock as directed in Henry Ford's will.

May 29. General Motors signed a contract with the U.A.W. providing for wages tied to a cost-of-living index.

June 15. The Tigers played the first night baseball game at Briggs Stadium.

October 6. Parking meters were installed on Detroit streets.

1949 The Detroit Symphony Orchestra was disbanded.

The United Foundation was established as the sole fund-raising campaign for all welfare and health agencies.

January 1. The Federal Government gave Fort Wayne to the city. It opened as a military museum on June 14, 1950, under the supervision of the Detroit Historical Commission.

September 29. The Ford Motor Company and the U.A.W. entered into a contract for worker pensions wholly financed by the Company. This was hailed as an outstanding labor relations event.

November 8. Albert E. Cobo, City Treasurer for seven terms, was elected Mayor.

December 30. Miss Mary V. Beck was sworn in as the first woman elected a member of the City Council.

1950 The population of Detroit was 1,849,568.

March 11. The Ford Motor Company Fund and the Ford and Lincoln-Mercury dealers presented a $2.5 million gift to the city for a Henry and Edsel Ford Memorial Auditorium as part of the Civic Center.

May 5. Ground was broken for the Douglas housing project.

May 6. The 102-day strike of the U.A.W. against the Chrysler Corporation ended with a $100 monthly pension agreement, but without a union-shop clause.

May 23. The United Auto Workers and General Motors Corporation agreed to a five-year contract including guaranteed annual wage increases, cost-of-living wage adjustments, a modified union shop and a $100 monthly pension at 65 after twenty-five years' service.

June 11. The Veterans' Memorial Building was opened as the first unit of the Civic Center.

July 19. Ground was broken for the Jeffries housing project.

1951 July 28. A mammoth parade depicting the history and development of Detroit climaxed the many festivities centering on Detroit's 250th anniversary.

April 18. Arthur H. Vandenberg, Republican Senator from Michigan since 1928, died. Blair Moody, a Detroit newspaperman, was appointed his successor.

April 21. The Detroit Street Railway Operators strike halted public transportation. It lasted 59 days until June 19.

October 18. The newly reactivated Detroit Symphony Orchestra gave its first concert.

1952 April 15. The Detroit Red Wings won the National League Hockey playoffs and the Stanley Cup.

1953 May 5. The Ford Motor Company celebrated its 50th anniversary.

November 3. Mayor Cobo was reelected.

1954 April 16. The Detroit Red Wings defeated Montreal to win the National Hockey League playoffs and the Stanley Cup.

May 13. President Dwight D. Eisenhower signed

the bill authorizing joint construction of the St. Lawrence Seaway with Canada.

1955 April 14. The Redwings defeated Montreal to win the Stanley Cup.

November 10. The Detroit United Foundation drive went over $14,450,000, which was said to be the world's largest collection.

December 12. The University of Detroit received a Ford Foundation grant.

1956 April 10. Montreal defeated the Redwings in the National Hockey League playoffs to win the Stanley Cup.

October 18. The Detroit Symphony Orchestra gave the first concert in the new Henry and Edsel Ford Auditorium.

December 8. United Auto Workers President Walter Reuther, in a letter to the city, proposed the formation of a municipal redevelopment corporation to rehabilitate industrial slums. He offered $10,000 from the Union treasury.

1957 September 12. Mayor Cobo died. City Council President Louis C. Miriani became Mayor on September 14.

November 5. Acting Mayor Louis C. Miriani was elected Mayor. Mary V. Beck became the first woman president of the City Council.

1958 March 10. Mayor Miriani announced plans of the City government to economize in the face of the recession.

March 25. Leon M. Wallace was named Director-Secretary of the Loyalty Investigating Committee. He was the first Negro to hold a city commission.

1959 January 28. Patrol car crews were racially integrated.

March 20. Plans for a twenty-three acre downtown redevelopment project were announced.

May 28. The <u>Detroit News</u> and the <u>Detroit</u>

Times raised their weekday price from 7 to 8 cents.

1960 The population of Detroit was 1,670,144.

May 31. Mayor Miriani vetoed a 1 % income tax bill, and the City Council failed to override it.

October 17. President Eisenhower received the key to the city and a miniature statue of the Spirit of Detroit.

November 7. The Detroit News acquired the Detroit Times.

December 28. The police were put on a six-day week.

1961 November 7. Jerome P. Cavanagh was elected Mayor. He was inaugurated January 2, 1962.

1962 A 1 % city income tax, sponsored by Mayor Cavanagh, was established.

December 1. The Civic Development Corporation announced plans to build a $57 million tourist and entertainment center near the downtown business district.

1963 September 9. Police Commissioner George Clifton Edwards, Jr. was appointed to the United States Appeals Court. His appointment was confirmed by the Senate on December 16.

November 26. Mayor Cavanagh and City Council President Carey proposed naming the old City Hall site for the late President John F. Kennedy, who was killed November 22.

1964 September 7. The area formerly occupied by the City Hall was renamed John F. Kennedy Plaza.

December 30. The National Association for the Advancement of Colored Peopel urged the Michigan Civil Rights Commission to study alleged police brutality against Negroes.

1965 April 3. The City along with Shreeveport, Louisiana, won the first AIA urban redevelopment award.

November 2. Mayor Cavanagh was reelected.

1967 March 23. A Negro boycott of the public schools in a protest against racism and a double standard of justice failed.

May. A drive to recall Mayor Cavanagh was shown to have strong racial overtones. Negro leaders rallied to the Mayor.

June 15. Patrolmen began a sick call to back the Police Officers Association demands for a pay raise. Some policemen were suspended. The POA and the patrolmen began to picket the station houses.

July 23. Thousands of Negroes rioted throughout a greater part of the city looting stores and throwing firebombs. As a result Governor Romney declared a state of emergency and ordered 1,500 National Guardsmen backed by tanks into the city to restore order. President Lyndon B. Johnson reluctantly sent 4,700 Army paratroopers into the city, which was paralyzed as a result of the disorders on July 24. The President addressed the nation indicating the gravity of the situation, which he believed could not be stopped by other methods. The major parts of the disturbances ended on July 26.

July 28. The National Guard and Army troops began to withdraw.

July 30. Federal troops were completely withdrawn and bivouaked at the State fairgrounds and city airport should another emergency arise calling for their return.

August 6. Governor Romney lifted the state of emergency.

August 15. Mayor Cavanagh and other city officials met with the Presidential Advisory Commission on Civil Disorders in Washington, D.C.

September 12. Governor Romney testified before the Presidential Advisory Commission on Civil Disorders repeating his charge that Federal assistance during the Detroit riot was too little and too late.

October 28. The study group, appointed by Mayor Cavanagh after the July riots, issued a report calling for a major overhaul of the government poverty programs and agencies. It urged creation of two super agencies, one to deal with human problems and one to handle physical renewal.

December 9. The City government presented a massive rebuilding program for 12th Street, the scene of the July riot. This reflected the views of those living in the area.

1968 January 4. Joseph L. Hudson, Jr., head of the New Detroit Committee seeking to plan and coordinate programs aimed at easing racial tensions in the city, announced that $100,000 matching Ford Doundation grants had been offered to rival Negro community groups: the Federation of Self-Determination headed by Rev. Albert B. Cleage, Jr. and the Detroit Council of Organizations led by Rev. Roy Allen.

March 6. Television station WXYZ-TV began using the word Afro-American rather than Negro in its broadcasting, indicating that it had received criticism for its use of the term Negro.

March 20. The pay of city policemen was raised from $8,335 to $10,000 per year, making it the highest in the country. The firemen received an equal increase.

April 5. A state of emergency was declared after scattered violence broke out in which a looter was killed by police, and two Negroes were shot by unknown persons. Governor Romney sent 3,000 National Guardsmen to the city, putting 6,000 more on alert. Mayor Cavanagh imposed a curfew. The rioting did not spread, and matters were calmed down in a few days.

May 6. The <u>Detroit Free Press</u> won a Pulitzer Prize for its reporting of the 1967 riots.

May 27. Mayor Cavanagh indicated that arrest or conviction for a felony would no longer nar men from joining the Police Department. This was part of a general revision of recruitment standards aimed at hiring more Negro policemen.

September 17. The Tigers won the American League Pennant.

October 10. The Tigers won the seventh and deciding game of the World Series defeating the St. Louis Cardinals.

December 30. The Detroit Common Council voted 6-2 in approving a Federal Model Cities program, which included a proposal for legalized prostitution in isolated areas of the city. The six backing the plan indicated their confidence that the latter provision would be removed later.

1969 February 7. An unarmed street patrol of Negro youths in semi-military clothing began to patrol high crime areas, as part of a program to attack problems in the Negro community.

March 30. One patrolman was killed and another injured when they approached a group of armed Negro men outside of the West Side New Baptist Church, where a meeting of a black separatist group called the Republic of New Africa had been held. Police then arrested 135 men inside the Church, all but ten of whom were freed by Judge George W. Crockett, Jr. R. Viers of New York who was suspected in the killing, surrendered to the FBI in New York City on April 18. He was arraigned on a first-degree murder charge on June 21. Viers and Clarence Fuller were acquitted in the slaying of Patrolman Michael Czapski on June 16, 1970.

June 24. Mayor Cavanagh announced that he would not run for reelection. Speculation grew that he knew that he would lose some Liberal and Black support because Richard H. Austin, a Negro, was running for the office.

November 4. Sheriff Roman S. Gribbs was elected Mayor by the narrowest margin in the city's history.

1970 The population of Detroit was 1,511,482.

March 7. The Urban Institute and the Detroit

Police Department announced an experiment in decentralized police patrolling. Under this plan, one sergeant would command twenty-one patrolmen having the responsibility for patrolling high crime rate areas.

June 28. New requirements for police officers were announced. They would have to have completed one year of college before taking promotion examinations as of September 1, 1973, and two years of college after September 1, 1796. No college training would be required before joining the force. The Department said it would pay tuition costs.

September 11. Police Commissioner Patrick V. Murphy was appointed New York City Police Commissioner by Mayor John V. Lindsay. John F. Nichols was named Detroit's new Police Commissioner on October 17.

October 24. One patrolman, Glenn Edwards, was killed, and another wounded in an exchange of gunfire near the headquarters of the National Committee to combat Fascism, a branch of the Black Panther Party.

1971 January 27. The Detroit Free Press announced a rise in price from ten to fifteen cents.

February 17. Sister Mary Margaret Slinger, principal of a Roman Catholic grade school, led the nuns on the staff in resigning their teaching posts. They charged the parents of the students with racism because of a recent vote by the St. Raymond Parish Council opposing the invitation of disadvantaged children from other areas to use the school's facilities. Archbishop Dearden supported the nuns.

September 3. The Kresge Company donated its headquarters to the Detroit Institute of Technology.

September 11. Mayor Roman S. Gribbs called for a statewide campaign to ban handguns in light of the increase of murders in the city.

September 27. District Court Judge Stephen J. Roth ruled that the city's school system had been deliberately segregated over a long period of time. The suit was brought by the NAACP.

October 4. A Federal Court ordered the Michigan Education Board to propose an integration plan for the metropolitan area including Detroit and some of its suburbs. A four month time limit was set. It also requested a report from the Detroit School Board on the progress of the magnet school plan which was to create special schools to draw students of all races to attend on a voluntary basis.

November 24. Henry Ford, president of the Ford Motor Company, announced that the Company's Land Development Corporation would build a $500-million complex of office buildings, retail stores and apartments in the downtown area of the city in order to help revitalize the area by luring people and businesses back to the inner city.

1972 March 9. Wayne County Sheriff's Deputy Henry S. Henderson was killed and Deputy Sheriffs James Jenkins, H. DuVall, and Aaron D. Vincent were wounded by gunfire as a result of a raid by three Detroit policemen on an apartment where the deputies were playing cards. The incident was called a "tragic mix-up." The policemen, members of the STRESS unit, were accused of shooting first.

May 22. Henry Ford 2nd announced at the Economic Club of Detroit that the redevelopment he had been planning for the downtown area would begin on a 32-acre riverfront site.

August 11. Three Detroit policemen: Virgil A. Starkey, James R. Harris and Ronald H. Martin, indicted on March 4 because of a shooting on March 9 of several sheriff's deputies, were acquitted.

October 3. The Tigers won the American League Eastern Division Championship.

October 12. The Oakland Athletics defeated the Tigers three games to two and won the American League Pennant.

1973 January 16. The U. S. Appeals Court, Sixth Circuit, agreed to rehear the full arguments on the school desegregation plan for Detroit and 52 suburban school districts. The court had ruled on December 8, 1972 that all the suburban school districts involved must have the opportunity to express their views in court.

February 8. The U. S. Appeals Court, Sixth District, nullified the decision of a three-judge panel upholding the principal of busing between Detroit and the suburbs. They would hear new arguments on the case and issue a new decision.

May 14. School custodial and service officials went on strike. One-third of the city's 10,500 teachers refused to cross the picket lines on May 15. The strike ended on May 16.

June 12. The Federal Appeals Court in Cincinnati ruled in a 6-3 decision that black children from Detroit had to ride buses to the suburbs and white children had to go to Detroit in order to achieve racial balance in the schools. The decision seemed to prepare the way for final determination by the U. S. Supreme Court on how far state and local areas would have to go in breaking down racial barriers in education.

September 4. The city's teachers went out on strike the day before the scheduled opening of classes.

October 15. The teachers voted to approve a new contract but would not return to work unless all fines levied on the teachers were removed. The teachers agreed to binding arbitration on key contract demands and returned to work on October 17.

November 6. State Senator Coleman A. Young was elected the first black mayor of Detroit, narrowly defeating former Police Commissioner John F. Nichols. A new city charter was also approved.

1974 February 27. U. S. Solicitor General Robert Bork, representing the Nixon Administration, asked the Supreme Court to reject the desegregation plan combining the predominantly black city schools with the predominantly white suburban schools into one metropolitan district because this would disrupt long-established government units.

March 8. Mayor Coleman A. Young disbanded the controversial anticrime STRESS unit because it was one of the main sources of racial problems in the city.

1975 May 20. City police officials made an agreement with the head of the Detroit Police Officers Association and the Lieutenants and Sergeants Association to prevent the layoff of 550 police officers whereby the officers would take fourteen days off without pay during the next year. The city would raise holiday compensation to 12 hours time off and give each officer an additional seven paid days off during the year. The Police Officers Association approved the agreement on June 11.

August 14. 700 sanitation truckdrivers, members of Teamsters' Local 214, struck. The strike ended on August 18.

August 16. U. S. District Court Judge Robert E. DeMascio rejected two desegregation proposals for the city school system and ordered development of a less sweeping plan. The NAACP indicated its intention to appeal the decision on August 19, claiming that Judge DeMascio was reacting to the concerns of the white power structure in the city.

October 14. Judge DeMascio extended the deadline for the submission of the school board's integration plan beyond October 15.

November 4. Judge DeMascio ruled that the city school system must begin an integration plan by January 26, 1976.

December 27. The Detroit Free Press raised its Sunday edition price from 35 to 50 cents.

1976 January 26. The court-ordered bussing of students began peaceably. Attendance was off by one-third but was near normal the next day.

March 20. Mayor Coleman A. Young announced plans to eliminate four city departments. Permanent and temporary lay-offs were announced. This action was taken in order to reduce the projected $44 million deficit by $2 million.

April 21. The city government began a three-day sale to sell city-owned junk which was collected for over sixty years. The items included old cobblestones and vintage fire trucks without engines or transmissions. This was to help reduce the projected huge deficit for the next year.

June 12. Mayor Young, acting to enforce an old statute requiring that city employees reside within the city, suspended several employees without pay. The majority were white policemen and firemen who indicated their intention to appeal the suspensions.

June 28. Mayor Young called for volunteers to fill some of the gaps in the police force because the city was facing massive layoffs of policemen.

July 2. In the midst of a massive sick-call protest over layoffs, Police Chief Philip G. Tannian threatened to dismiss those police officers who were insistent upon continuing their protest.

August 16. As a result of an attack upon spectators at a Rock Concert the city government recalled 450 laid-off police officers.

September 28. Mayor Young named William L. Hart as the city's first black police chief to replace Philip Tannian who was dismissed.

October 26. Mayor Young formed an Economic Growth Council to reorganize city government operations and the tax structure to help the city face its fiscal and job crises. Retired Chrysler Corporation Chairman Lynn Townsend and retired General Motors Corporation Chairman James Riche were appointed co-chairmen of the council.

DOCUMENTS

The documents in this section have been carefully selected to illustrate the social, political, commercial and cultural life of Detroit, as well as the central position of the city in regard to trade via the Great Lakes chain from the early eighteenth century through the 1960's. The most pertinent items from the Ordinances, Charters and Reports of various agencies and departments of the city have been chosen to indicate the major changes which have occurred in the governance of Detroit. The city has played a major role in the industrial development of the United States during the twentieth century because of the development of the automobile industry. The major companies still have their headquarters in the area. Studies of housing, recreational facilities and industrial reconstruction as well as core-city redevelopment are included. Descriptions of the city at important periods in its development are also included. Obviously much more could have been included, but the most important documents were selected due to the limited space.

DETROIT IN 1778-1779

The following description of Detroit during the Revolutionary War was given by James May who died in 1829. He indicates the military disposition of the town as well as the residential area. In addition the relationships and trade with the Indians is discussed. The administration of justice is also described. This indicates the growth and potential of the town.

Source: Sketches of the City of Detroit, State of Michigan. Past and Present, 1855. Detroit, 1855, pp. 5-9.

[Taken from Hon. Alexander D. Fraser]

The following narrative was taken down from the lips of James May, Esq. my father-in-law, who died in January, 1829. He was an Englishman who came to this place when a young man in 1778. He was Chief Justice of Common Pleas, established here immediately after General Wayne took possession of the Country, under Jay's Treaty; was Colonel of Militia, &c. . . .

A.D.F.

My Note Book, 1826

In the year 1778, after a passage of four days from Fort Erie, I arrived by the brig-of-war Genl. Gage, at the settlement of Detroit. No vessels at that time navigated upon the lakes, upon account of the revolutionary war which then raged, except those of His Majesty--not even, but few vessels ever visited the lakes, and those very few and of an inferior class--indeed, no merchant vessel had as yet ploughed the waves of the lakes.

The old town of Detroit comprised within its limits that space between Mr. Palmer's store (Conant Block) and Capt. Perkins' house (near the Arsenal Building), and extended back as far as the public barn, and in front was bordered by the Detroit River. It was an oblong square; and covered about two acres in length, and an acre and a half in breadth. It was surrounded with oak and cedar pickets about fifteen feet long. The town had four gates, east, west, north and south. Over the first three of these gates were block houses. Each of these had four guns (six-pounders each). The first of these was in that space intervening between Palmer's shop and Judge Poor's house (opposite Ives' bank.) . . . There were besides two gun batteries fronting the river, and in a parallel direction with the block-houses. There were streets that run east and west; the main street was twenty feet wide and the rest fifteen feet wide. There were three cross streets, running north and south from ten to fifteen feet wide. At that time there was no fort, but there was a citadel on the ground on which Perkins' house now stands, (N.W. corner of Jefferson avenue and Wayne street,) the pump of which still remains there. The citadel was picketed in, and within it were erected barracks of wood, two stories high, sufficient to contain ten offices; and there were barracks sufficient to maintain from three to four hundred men; a provision store built of brick. There was also within the citadel an hospital and guard house.

In the town of Detroit, in the year 1778, there was about sixty houses, most of them one story high, and a few of them a story and a half; but none of them were two stories. They were all of logs, some hewn and some round. There was also a building of a splendid appearance, called the King's Palace. It was two stories high. It was situated near the east gate, and stood where Conant's new building (Beecher's store) now stands. The pump which now stands behind that building stood in the rear of the Government House. Attached to this house was a large garden extending towards the river which contained many fruit trees. When I first came here it was occupied by Governor Hamilton, for whom it was built. He was the first Governor commissioned here by the British Government, and was here about three years before I came. There were four companies of the Eighth Regiment, two companies of Butler's Rangers, and one Company of the Fourth Regiment. The latter was under the command of Capt. Anbey, the former under Capt. Caldwell, and Eighth Regiment commanded by Major Leverault, who was also commanding officer of the post and its dependencies. All these constituted about five hundred troops. There was a guard house near the west gate, and another near the Government House. Each of these guards consisted of twenty-four, and a subaltern officer, who mounted regularly every morning between nine and ten o'clock. Each of these guards furnished four sentinels who relieved every two hours. There was also an officer of the day who did strict duty. All these gates were shut at 9 o'clock regularly, and the keys delivered into the hands of the commanding officer. They were opened in the morning at sunrise. No Indian whatever, or squaw was permitted to enter the town with any instrument, such as a tomahawk, or even knife.. . . No more than twenty-five Indians were allowed to come into the town at the same time--they were permitted to come in only at the east and west gates. At sun-set the drum beat, and all the Indians were compelled to leave town instantly. . . .

There was a Council House, for the purpose of holding council with the Indians. It was near the water side, rear of the Government House. There was a Roman Catholic Church situated where Payne's brick house now stands (near the Masonic Hall.) The priest was then Peter Simple, an aged and infirm man, and adjoining it was the Priest's house and burying ground. The church was 60 by 40 feet, one story high, with two steeples and two bells.

The population of the town was sixty families, in all about two hundred males and one hundred females. They--the men--were chiefly bachelors. There was not a marriage in the place for a number of years, until I broke the ice. Twenty of these persons were traders and kept retail stores. Of the population there were 30 Scotchmen, 4 Englishmen and 15 Irishmen.

The extent of the settlement up the Detroit River reached about Hudson's House (now Fisher's) not a house above that place in this country, . . .

The Indian trade was then excellent. There was much public money then in circulation here, for the troops and the Navy Department, were then strong here. This post was established by the British to keep the Indians in check, of whom they were afraid; and this was the reason why the old town was built so compact, that it might in case of urgency be most able to defend it against the assaults of the Indians. The different tribes were the Hurons, Wyandotts, Chippewas and Pottawattamies, Taways and the Moravians. Frequently between 3 and 500 of these could be seen at a time during the revolutionary war. The civil department consisted of two Justices of the Peace, one of them was the late Thomas Williams Esq., . . and the other was the Governor or commanding officer, for the time. The Orderly Sergeant was the Constable. The Justice kept the peace, and the commanding officer took cognizance of all cases under £ 10 York. For all sums above this, writs came from Montreal, addressed to Williams, who got his Bailiff to execute them. -- In case of small debts, on a complaint to the commanding officer, he sent his orderly to the debtor requesting his immediate attendance before that officer. He would then hear the parties and make his determination accordingly. If against the defendant, he would order him instantly to pay the money, or send him to the Guard House until he complied, and some times would give him a little time to pay; there was no process or costs in these cases. If the debtor, however, had no property, the party was set at liberty. One Granchin owed me a debt. I complained to Gov. Hamilton, who sent for him. He came, and being asked if he had anything to say against the debt, he said no. He then ordered him to give me a negro wench in payment, and she served me twenty-five years.

* * *

INCORPORATION OF THE TOWN OF DETROIT
February 19, 1802

The Territorial Legislature incorporated "the Town of Detroit" providing for its governance by five Trustees, a Secretary, an Assessor, a Collector, and a Town Marshal. Provisions for local control, and legislation by the Board of Trustees were made. Residents were to determine the amount of taxes to be collected. Judicial regulations were also established.

Source: Corporation of the Town of Detroit. Act of Incorporation and Journal of the Board of Trustees. Detroit, 1922, pp. 3-7.

An Act to Incorporate The Town of Detroit

Sec. 1st. BE it enacted by the legislative Council & house of Representatives in general assembly, and it is hereby enacted by the authority of the Same that Such parts of the townships of Detroit and Hamtramck in the County of WAYNE, as are contained in the following boundaries & limits, to wit; bounded in front by the River or Strait of Detroit, Eastwardly by the division line between John Askin Esqr. and Antoine Bobien--Westwardly by the division line between the farm belonging to the Heirs of the late William McComb deceased, and Pierre Chene, and extending back from Said river two miles, at an equal Width in rear, as in front, and including all Wharves & buildings in front of Said town, be and the Same are hereby erected into a town Corporate which Shall henceforth be Known and distinguished by the Name of "THE TOWN of DETROIT."

Sec. 2. AND be it further enacted that of the better ordering and regulating the police of Said town of Detroit & the Inhabitants thereof, there Shall henceforth be in Said town five Trustees, a Secretary, an Assessor, a Collector, and a Town Marshal, who Shall be Inhabitants of Said town, and who Shall be Chosen, as hereinafter mentioned. The Trustees Shall be a body politic in law by the Name of "THE BOARD of TRUSTEES of the town of Detroit" one of whom Shall act as Chairman of Said board, and one as treasurer, to be appointed by Said trustees, any three of Said Trustees Shall Constitute a board for business, the Secretary being present.

Sec. 3. AND BE IT FURTHER ENACTED that the Said Trustees and their Successors in office Shall be able in their Corporate Capacity and for the use of Said Corporation, to receive, acquire, hold & convey any Estate, real or personal, and Shall also be Capable, in law by their Corporate Name aforesaid of Suing & being Sued, of pleading and being impleaded in any action or Suit, real or personal, in any Court of record whatever, and they are hereby authorised to have & use one Common Seal for the purposes of Said Corporation, and the Same to alter, break, or renew at their discretion.

Sec. 4. AND BE IT FURTHER ENACTED that the Inhabitants of Said town of Detroit, who are freeholders, or householders paying an annual rent of forty dollars, and Such other persons residing within Said town, who Shall be admitted to the freedom of Said Corporation by a Majority of the Electors at their annual Meetings, Shall & may assemble at Such place, within Said town, as Shall be pointed out by a Majority of the Said Trustees, on the first Monday of May yearly and every year, and there elect by the highest Number of Votes of the Electors present five discreet & Suitable persons resident within Said Corporation to Serve as Trustees of Said town for one year next ensuing, and untill other trustees are chosen & qualified; also a Secretary, an Assessor, a Collector, and a town Marshal, who Shall Serve for a like term of time.--the Trustees and all other officers of Said Corporation Shall within ten days after notice of their respective appointments take an oath or affirmation faithfully and impartially to execute & discharge the duties of their Said offices before Some persons in Said County authorised to administer oaths, a certificate whereof Shall be given to the person taking the oath, and by him filed with the Secretary of Said board.

Sec. 5. AND be it further enacted that the Said Trustees, when convened for business, Shall be called "THE BOARD OF TRUSTEES OF THE TOWN OF DETROIT" and they or any three of them, Shall have full power and authority from time to time, and at any time, to hold a meeting in Said town, at Such place as the Chairman or in his absence the Secretary Shall point out, and to make, ordain, & establish in writing Such laws and ordinances, and the Same from time to time to alter or repeal, as to them Shall Seem necessary and proper, for the health, Safety, cleanliness, Convenience and good government of Said Town of Detroit, and the Inhabitants thereof; to appoint a Treasurer of their own body, to administer all the necessary oaths, to impose reasonable fines, penalties & forfeitures upon all persons who Shall offend against the laws & ordinances that Shall be So made as aforesaid, and to levy and cause to be Collected all Such fines & forfeitures by warrant of the Chairman with the Seal of Said Corporation directed to the Marshall who is hereby authorised & directed to Collect the Same by distress & Sales of the goods & chatters of the offender, and the Same to pay to the treasurer to & for the use of Said Corporation; and it Shall [be] the further and particular duty of the Said board of Trustees to make, adopt and establish regulations for Securing Said Town against injuries from fires, to cause the Streets, lanes and alleys of Said town, and the public Commons to be kept open & in repairs and free from every Kind of nuisances, to regulate markets, and if necessary, to appoint a clerk of the market, to regulate the assize of bread, both as to weight & price, having due regard at all times, in establishing the Same, to the market price and value of flour in Said town; and to prevent Swine and other animals from running at large in the Streets, alleys and on the public Commons of Said town, if in their opinion the interest or Convenience of Said town Shall require Such prohibition; all Such laws, ordinances, and regulations So to be made Shall be in force and binding from thenceforth untill the next annual meeting for the election of Corporate officers, when all laws, regulations, and ordinances made, adopted, and in force under the authority of this act Shall be by the Secretary of Said board laid before the electors of Said town for their Consideration, and if any of Said laws, rules & regulations made & adopted by the Said board of Trustees for the good Government and Well being of Said Corporation, Shall be disapproved of and rejected by a Majority of the Voters present, the Said laws, ordinances, and regulations So disapproved of Shall thenceforth become Null and Void and of no effect; provided that the laws & ordinances So to be made by the board of trustees as aforesaid, Shall be Consistent with the laws & ordinances of the Territory.

Sec. 6. AND be it further enacted that the freeholders, householders, and residents aforesaid of Said town Shall at their annual Meeting have the power and authority to vote Such Sum or Sums of money as a Majority of Such Voters present may think proper to be raised, for the use of the Said town for the ensuing year, which Sum or Sums money So voted Shall be assessed by the Assessor in Such Manner, upon Such objects, and in Such proportion, as Shall be agreed upon by a Majority of Such meeting, and Shall be Collected by the Collector at Such times, and be paid & disposed of in Such manner as the board of trustees Shall direct, and Said Collector Shall have the Same power to Compel payment, as is or Shall be given to County Collectors, for the Collection of County votes and levies.

Sec. 7. AND be it further enacted that the board of trustees Shall have the power of filling all Vacancies that may happen in any of the offices that are herein established and made elective and the appointments So made Shall Continue Valid untill the next annual Meeting and no longer. . .

FIRE ORDINANCE, February 25, 1802

Concern over the danger of fire in the early nineteenth century led the newly formed Board of Trustees to pass the following legislation as a preventive measure. Chimnies were to be inspected and properly cleaned. Householders were to be careful with warm ashes, provide water buckets for fire fighting, and turn out to help put out fires. Limits were also placed on the maintenance of gun powder.

Source: Corporation of the Town of Detroit. Act of Incorporation and Journal of the Board of Trustees, 1802-1805. Detroit, 1922, pp. 10-13.

AN ORDINANCE made & established on the twenty fifth day of February A.D. 1802 by the board of Trustees of the town of Detroit for the better Securing of the Said town against injuries of fire.

Art. 1st. That all Chimnies found insufficient, Shall be immediately repaired, in deffault of which the person or persons, who Shall make use of them, after one week's notice of their insufficience, Shall, on oath of one creditable Witness forfeit five dollars, or any lesser Sum, at the discretion of the board of trustees.

Art. 2. That all Chimnies, where fire is Kept Shall be Swept on/c/e in every two weeks from the last Saturday in October to the last Saturday in April, and once in every four Weeks through the remaining part of the year; the Sweeping to be performed on Saturday before nine o'clock in the Morning; and person or persons neglecting the Same Shall forfeit three dollars each time, or any lesser Sum at the discretion of the Trustees,

Art. 3. That the person or persons, whose Chimnies Shall take fire, Shall forfeit, for each time, ten dollars or any lesser Sum at the discretion of the board of Trustees. . . .

Art. 11. That no person within the limits of the picketts, Keep, or have at any one time more than a Keg or half barrell of gunpowder, in his house, lodging, or other place in the town (the powder Magazin excepted) under the penalty of twenty five dollars and forfeiting the Surplus powder So found; . . .

Art. 12. That on the first alarm of fire all the male Inhabitants of the town, except those before appointed, are required to form a line for the Supply of Water from the river to the fire, following Such directions as they will afterwards receive from the Trustees, . . .

ESTABLISHMENT OF THE MERCHANTS' WHARF
July 16, 1804

As part of the attempts to provide additional commercial advantages for Detroit, the newly organized Board of Trustees passed an ordinance regulating the wharf and establishing fees. James Abbott was appointed supervisor of the dock with provisions made for payment of his salary at a certain percent of the fees collected.

Source: Corporation of the Town of Detroit. Act of Incorporation and Journal of the Board of Trustees, 1802-1805. Detroit, 1922, pp. 66-67.

AN ORDINANCE made & established by the board of Trustees of the Corporation of the town of Detroit this Sixteenth day of July A.D. 1804; to regulate the Warfage of the Corporation Warf, Commonly Called the Merchants' Warf;

WHEREAS Considerable expences have been incurred by the Corporation of Detroit, in the repairs of what has been Commonly Called the Merchants' warf: and Whereas a constant attention, and also an occasional expenditure of money will be necessary to Keep Said Warf in a State Suitable for the lading and unlading of goods, and to answer the ordinary purposes of the town, the board of Trustees of the Corporation of the town of Detroit ordain, fix, and establish the following rates viz.

Each & every vessell of, or above 20 tons burthen, to be paid on her arrival, without reference to the particular object of her Coming. $1. 50

Each & every batteau, in like manner . . . " 25

Each & every perogue or canoe, in like manner " 12½

Each & every freeholder, tenant, or heads of family desirous of getting their water from Said Warf, annually in advance. 1. 0

with this exception nevertheless, that during the market-hours of those market days established by this board, no warfage Shall be collected from boats, perogues, canoes, or other Small crafts coming to market with the produce of the Country.

Sec. 2d. That James Abbott esq^{r}. be appointed to Superintend the observance of this ordinance: that it Shall be his duty to cause Such repairs to be made to the warf aforesaid, as this board Shall from time to time direct; and that he be allowed five per Cent on the Collection of all warfage money: that he Keep fair accounts of receipt and expenditures, . . .

TRAVEL ON THE LAKE VIA "THE WALK-IN-THE-WATER," 1818-1821

This is a description of the first trip of the first steamboat, "The Walk-In-The-Water" from Buffalo to Detroit in September, 1818, and details of the fatal voyage which led to the wreck of the steamship in November, 1821. Indications are given of the type of accomodations available and the difficulties which ensued when the disaster occurred.

Source: Friend Palmer. Early Days in Detroit. Papers Written by General Friend Palmer of Detroit. Being His Personal Reminiscences of Important Events and Descriptions of the City for Over Eighty Years. Detroit, 1904. pp. 84-85, 88-93.

The Detroit Gazette of that day said of her first trip to this city:

"The Walk-in-the-Water left Buffalo at one and a half P. M. and arrived at Dunkirk at thirty-five minutes past 6 on the same day. On the following morning she arrived at Erie, Captain Fish having reduced her steam in order not to pass that place, where he took in a supply of wood. The boat was visited by all the inhabitants during the day, and had the misfortune to get aground for a short time in the bay, a little west of French Street. At half past 7 P. M. she left Erie and arrived at Cleveland at 11 o'clock. Tuesday at twenty minutes past 6 o'clock P. M. she sailed and reached Sandusky bay at 1 o'clock on Wednesday; lay at anchor during the night, and then proceeded to Venice for wood; left Venice at 3 P. M. and arrived at the mouth of the Detroit River, where she anchored during the night. The whole time of the first voyage from Buffalo to Detroit occupied forty-four hours and ten minutes--the wind being ahead during the whole passage. Not the slightest accident happened during the voyage, and her machinery worked admirably.

"Nothing could exceed the surprise of the 'sons of the forest' on seeing the Walk-in-the-Water move majestically and rapidly against wind and current, without sails or oars. Above Maiden they lined the shores and expressed their astonishment by repeated shouts of 'Taiyoh nichee!' (An exclamation of surprise.)

"A report that had circulated among them that a 'big canoe' would soon come from the 'noisy waters,' which by order of the 'great father of the "Chemo Komods"' (Long knives, or Kankees), would be drawn through the lakes and rivers by a sturgeon. Of the truth of this report they were perfectly satisfied.

"Her second arrival at Detroit was on September 7 of the same year, having on board thirty-one passengers, including the Earl of Selkirk and suite, destined for the far northwest.

"The cabins of the Walk-in-the-Water were fitted up in a neat, convenient style, and a trip from Buffalo was considered not only tolerable, but truly pleasant. . . .

WRECK OF THE WALK-IN-THE-WATER

"On Wednesday last the steamboat Walk-in-the-Water left Black Rock at 4 P.M. on her regular trip to Detroit; the weather though somewhat rainy, did not appear threatening. After she had proceeded about four miles above Bird Island she was struck by a severe squall, which it was immediately perceived had injured her much and caused her to leak fast. The wind from the southwest continued to blow with extreme severity through the night, which was exceedingly dark and rainy, attended at intervals with the most tremendous squalls. The lake became rough to a terrifying degree and every wave seemed to threaten immediate destruction to the boat and all on board. This was truly to the passengers and crew a night of terror and dismay--to go forward was impossible; to attempt to return to Black Rock in the darkness and tempest would have been certain ruin, on account of the difficulty of the channel; and little less could be hoped, whether the boat were anchored, and for awhile held fast, but as every one perceived, each wave increased her injury and caused her to leak faster; the casings in her cabin were seen to move at every swell, and the squeaking of her joints and timbers was appalling; her engine was devoted to the pumps, but in spite of them all the water increased to an alarming extent--the storm grew more terrible. The wind blew more violently as the night advanced, and it was presently perceived that she was dragging her anchors and approaching the beach. In such blackness of darkness could her helm have commanded her course, not the most skillful pilot could have chosen with any certainty the part of the shore on which it would be most prudent to land. The passengers on board were numerous and many of them were ladies, whose fears and cries were truly heartrending.

"In this scene of distress and danger, the undersigned passengers in the boat, fell that an expression of the warmest gratitude is due to Captain J. Rogers, for the prudence, coolness and intelligence with which he discharged his duty; his whole conduct evinced that he was capable and worthy of his command. . . . No less credit is due to the other officers, Sailing Master Miller, and Engineer Calhoun, and even the whole crew. . . . she beached . . . above the light house, . . .

HENRY SCHOOLCRAFT'S DESCRIPTION OF DETROIT, 1820

Henry Schoolcraft kept a journal of his travels through the Northwest during 1820. The expedition arrived in Detroit on May 8, and left on May 24, 1820. He presented a detailed description of the mild climate in May. This selection illustrates certain aspects of the voyage from Buffalo to Detroit and the care which Schoolcraft took in his narrative.

Source: Henry R. Schoolcraft. Narrative Journal of Travels Through the Northwestern Regions of the United States Extending From Detroit Through the Great Chain of American Lakes, To The Sources of the Mississippi River. Performed as a Member of the Expedition Under Governor Cass. In the Year 1820. Albany, 1821, pp. 71-72.

* * *

With respect to the climate of Detroit, the result of our observations will allow us to speak in a very favourable manner. Situated in the longitude of Chillicothe, in Ohio, and on the parallel of latitude which embraces Prarie du Chien, on the Mississippi, and Albany, on the Hudson, it falls under that temperate medium of climate, which is found so favourable to the cereal gramine. the grasses and the fruit trees of the United States. This we first witnessed in the early development of Spring, always one of the best tests of the benignity of a climate. On leaving Buffalo, on the 6th of May, the blossoms of the peach tree were not yet fully expanded, and the petals of the apple were just beginning to swell. On reaching Detroit, two days afterwards, the leaves of the peach blossom had fallen, and those of the apple had passed the heighth of their bloom. Gardening also, which had not commenced at Buffalo, we found finished at Detroit, and the half grown leaves of the beach, the maple, the common hickory, . . . , and to the fields the delightful appearance of Spring. These facts will go farther in determining upon the differences of climate, then meteorological registers, which only indicate the state of the atmosphere, without noticing whether a corresponding effect is produced upon vegetation. During ten days of the period of our detention at Detroit, of which I kept a meteorological register, the mean daily temperature of the atmosphere, (for a period of ten days,) as indicated by a Fahrenheit thermometer was 61°. . . .

NEW CITY CHARTER, April 4, 1827

The City of Detroit had been governed under a system of a Board of Trustees since its incorporation in 1802. After careful consideration the citizens and the legislature decided that it would be best to reorganize the municipal administration under the name of "The Mayor, Recorder, Aldermen and Freemen of the City of Detroit." This selection was taken from the revised Charter of 1848.

Source: The Revised Charter and Ordinances of the City of Detroit. Detroit, 1848, pp. 5-9.

AN ACT relative to the City of Detroit, approved April 4, 1827

Sec. 1. Be it enacted by the Legislative Council of the Territory of Michigan, That the district of country contained within the following limits, . . . shall continue to be a city by the name of the "City of Detroit;" and all the freemen of said city, from time to time, being inhabitants thereof, shall be, and continue to be, a body corporate and politic, by the name of "The Mayor, Recorder, Aldermen and Freemen, of the City of Detroit," and by that name, they and their successors shall be known in law, and shall be, and are hereby made, capable of suing and being sued, of pleading and being impleaded, of answering and being answered unto, and of defending and being defended, in all Courts of Record, and any other place whatsoever; and may have a common seal, and may change and alter the same at their pleasure; and by the same name shall be, and are hereby made capable of purchasing, holding, conveying, and disposing of any real and personal estate, for the use of said corporation.

Sec. 2. There shall be the following officers in and for the said city, to wit: One mayor, one Recorder, five Aldermen one Clerk, one Marshal, one Treasurer, one Supervisor, one Assessor, one Collector, and three constables of whom the Mayor, Recorder and Aldermen shall be freeholders.

Sec. 3. That the freemen of the said city, having the qualifications of electors of members of the Legislative Council, and having resided within the said city one year, next preceding the election, and at the same time residing therein, shall, on the first Monday in April, in every year, . . . shall elect one Mayor, five Aldermen, one Supervisor, one Assessor, one Marshall. . .

INCORPORATION OF FIRE DEPARTMENT
February 14, 1840

The fire department was organized as a tontine company to provide for effective fire fighting, as well as necessary care for the indigent and disabled firemen and their families. Provisions were also made for the company to hold property necessary to its work. The Supreme Court eventually declared this company to be unconstitutional.

Source: The Revised Charter and Ordinances of the City of Detroit. Detroit, 1848, pp. 57-59.

AN ACT to incorporate the Fire Department of the City of Detroit.

Whereas, the members of an Association, known as the "Fire Department of the city of Detroit," have petitioned the Legislature to grant them an act of incorporation, to enable them the more effectually to acconplish the objects of their organization, and to provide means for the relief of disabled firemen and their families; therefore,

Sec. 1. Be it enacted by the Senate and House of Representatives of the State of Michigan, That all persons who now are, or may hereafter become, members of the Fire Department of the city of Detroit, and their successors, shall be and hereby are ordained, constituted, and declared to be, and continue, a body of politic and corporate, in fact and in name, under the name and style of "The Fire Department of the city of Detroit," for the purposes recited in above preamble, and by that name they and their successors may and shall have perpetual succession, and shall be known in law, capable of suing and being sued, of pleading and being impleaded, of answering and being answered unto, of defending and being defended, in all suits, complaints, matters, causes, courts and places whatsoever, and both in law and equity; and capable of having a common seal; of acquiring by purchase, gift, devise, or otherwise, and of holding and conveying any real, personal, or mixed estate, necessary, proper or expedient for the objects of this incorporation; Provided, That the amount of said estate shall at no time exceed the sum of thirty thousand dollars.

Sec. 2. The members of the Fire Department of the city of Detroit, hereby incorporated, shall have, and are hereby declared to have, full power and authority to make and prescribe such by-laws, rules, ordinances and regulations, and the same to alter, amend and change at pleasure, as to them, from time to time, shall seem needful or proper, touching the management and disposition of their funds for the objects aforesaid; touching the regular and special meetings of the Department; the regulation, duty and conduct of their members, delegates and board of trustees; the election and displacing of officers and delegates; the admission and expulsion of members; the filling of vacancies in offices; and touching every other matter and thing necessary or expedient for the good government and promotion of this incorporation, or which appertains to the business and objects for which the said incorporation is, by this act, instituted; Provided, That such by-laws, rules, ordinances and regulations, be not repugnant to the Constitutional laws of the United States, or of this State.

Sec. 3. The officers of said Department by this act incorporated, shall be a President, Vice President, Secretary, Treasurer, and Collector, who, together with the Chief Engineer of the Fire department, and the Delegates from the several Fire Companies, and other bodies, pursuant to the provisions of the Constitution and by-laws of the Department, shall constitute a board of trustees, a majority of whom shall be a quorum for the transaction of business; and said officers and delegates, separately, and as a board of trustees, shall do and perform such duties and things as may be incumbent upon, or required of, them by the Constitution or by-laws of the Department.

Sec. 4. There shall be an annual meeting of the members of said corporation on the third Monday of January, in each year, at which the officers shall be elected by ballot, by a majority of the members present, from their own body. And the officers elected shall hold their offices for one year, or until others be chosen in their places; . . .

FREE SCHOOLS ACT, February 17, 1842

This act provided for the establishment of school inspectors, and a Board of Education. The Board was given power and authority to make by-laws and ordinances, and regulate the school attendance age. Provisions were also made for collection and disbursement of funds for education.

Source: The Revised Charter and Ordinances of the City of Detroit. Detroit, 1848, pp. 50-53.

AN ACT relative to Free Schools in the city of Detroit.

SEC. 1. Be it enacted by the Senate and House of Representatives of the State of Michigan. That the city of Detroit shall be considered as one school district, and hereafter all schools organized therein, in pursuance of this act, shall, under the direction and regulations of the Board of Education, be public and free to all children residing within the limits thereof, between the ages of five and seventeen years, inclusive.

SEC. 2. In lieu of the school inspectors now required to be elected in said city, there shall be twelve school inspectors, to be elected in the manner following: At the next annual charter election, there shall be elected in each ward of said city, two school inspectors, one of whom shall hold his office for two years, and the other for one year; and at every annual (charter) election thereafter, there shall be elected in each ward, one school inspector, who shall hold his office for two years. No school inspector shall be entitled to receive any compensation for his services.

SEC. 3. In case of a vacancy in the office of school inspector, the Common Council of the city of Detroit may fill the same, until the next annual election, when, if such vacancy happen in the first year of the term of said office, the electors of the proper ward may choose a suitable person to fill the remainder of such term: Provided, The city clerk shall give notice of such vacancy prior to such election, as may be required in other cases.

SEC. 4. Every person elected to the office of school inspector, who, without sufficient cause, shall neglect or refuse to serve, shall forfeit to the board of education for the use of the library, the sum of ten dollars, to be recovered in an action of debt in some competent court; Provided, no person shall be compelled to serve two terms successively; and the said board shall make all necessary rules and regulations relative to its proceedings, and punish by fine, not exceeding five dollars for each offense of any member of the board, who may, without sufficient cause, absent himself from any meeting thereof, to be collected as they may direct.

SEC. 5. The school inspectors, together with the Mayor and Recorder of said city, (who are declared to be ex-officio school inspectors,) shall be a body corporate, by the name and style of "the Board of Education of the city of Detroit," and in that name may be capable of suing and being sued, and of holding or selling and conveying real and personal property, as the interest of said common schools may require; and shall also succeed to, and be entitled to demand all moneys and other rights belonging to or in possession of the board of school inspectors, or any member thereof, or of any school district board, or any member thereof, or any real and personal property, or other rights, of any such district in said city, and the clear proceeds of all such property which may come into the possession of said board, as last aforesaid. . . .

SEC. 6. The Board of Education. . . may meet from time to time at such place in said city as they may designate; the Mayor shall be President of the Board and shall preside at all meetings thereof, but in case of his absence, or the absence of the Recorder, a majority of the inspectors present at any meeting, may choose one of their number President pro tempore.

SEC. 7. The Clerk of the said city shall be ex-officio Clerk of said Board, and shall perform such duties as the Board of Education may reasonable require. In case of the absence of said Clerk, or for any other cause, the Board may choose some suitable person to perform his duties, either as principal or deputy Clerk.
. . .

SEC. 9. The Board of Education shall have full power and authority, and it shall be their duty to purchase such school houses, and apply for and receive from the County Treasurer, or other officer, all moneys appropriated for the Primary Schools and District Library of said city, and designate a place where the Library may be kept therein. The said Board shall also have full power and authority to make by-laws and ordinances relative to taking the census of all children in said city between the ages of five and seventeen years; relative to making all necessary reports, and transmitting the same to the proper offices, as designated by law, so that said city may be entitled to its proportion of the Primary School fund; relative to visitation of schools; relative to the length of time schools shall be kept, which shall not be less than three months in each year; relative to the employment and examination of teachers, their powers and duties; relative to the regulation of schools and the books to be used therein; relative to the appointment of necessary officers, and prescribe their powers and duties; relative to anything whatever that may advance the interest of education, the good government and prosperity of Common Schools in said city, and the welfare of the public concerning the same.

SEC. 10. The Mayor's Court shall have jurisdiction of all suits wherein said Board may be a party, and of all prosecutions for violation of said By-laws and Ordinances.

SEC. 11. The said Board shall annually, in the month of February, publish in some newspaper of the city, the number of schools in said city, the number of pupils instructed therein the year preceding, the several branches of education pursued by them, and the expenditures for all things authorized by this act, during the preceding year.

SEC. 12. The Board of Education shall establish a district library, and for the increase of the same, the Common Council are authorized annually to lay a tax on the real and personal property within said city, of a sum not exceeding two hundred dollars, which tax shall be levied and collected in the same manner as the moneys raised to defray the general expenditures of said city.

SEC. 13. The Common Council of said city are hereby authorized, once in each year to assess and levy a tax on all the real and personal property within said city, according to the city assessment roll of that year, which shall not exceed one dollar for every child in said city between the ages of five and seventeen years; the number of children to be ascertained by the last report on that subject, on file in the office of the Clerk of the county of Wayne, or in the office of the Clerk of said Board of Education, and certified by the President thereof, and the said tax shall be collected in the same manner as the moneys raised to defray the general expenses of said city; all such moneys shall be disbursed and expended by the authority of said Board, for the support and maintenance of said schools, and for no other purpose whatever.

***

ADMISSION OF NEGRO CHILDREN TO PUBLIC SCHOOLS, 1869

Detroit had maintained separate schools for white and black children. However, with the pressure of the Reconstruction era and the amendments to the Constitution as well as the decision of the Supreme Court, the city had to admit the colored children to the public schools. The President of the Board of Education explained the background for this change in his annual report.

Source: Detroit. Education Board. Twenty-seventh Annual Report of the Board of Education for the Year Ending December 31, 1869. Detroit, 1870.

To the Members of the Board of Education of the City of Detroit:

* * *

Admission of Colored Children

During the year an important change has been made in regard to the admission of colored children into the schools under the charge of the Board. From the commencement of our school system separate schools had been maintained for colored children, and no provision has ever been made, or opportunity, under our system, afforded them for advancing higher than the junior grade. This had been a just ground for complaint on the part of our colored citizens for many years, and it was manifestly unjust to them, "for a true system of free schools should afford equal advantage to all."

As there was a difference of opinion among the members of the Board, not only in reference to the propriety of a change in the previous practices, but also in regard to a proper construction of the law touching the subject, the hindrances existing in our rules and regulations to the admission of colored children in to our schools upon an equal footing with others were not rescinded until after the decision of the Supreme Court in the case of Workman vs. the Board of Education in April last. This decision established the right of the colored child to admission, under the law, into our schools on perfectly equal terms with all others. In compliance with the law, as affirmed by this decision of the Supreme Court, the Board rescinded all rules and regulations assigning them to separate schools, and colored children are now admitted to all the schools. . .

REVISED CITY CHARTER, June 7, 1883
AS AMENDED IN 1895

The City Charter was revised with so many amendments in 1883 that it was virtually a new law. The powers of the municipal officers and other administrative regulations were further amended in 1895 and in the following years. Selections below indicate the provisions for election of the municipal officials and their rights, powers and duties.

Source: The Charter of the City of Detroit With Amendments Thereto and the Acts of the Legislature Relating to or Affecting the City of Detroit. Detroit, 1904. pp. 3-5, 73-75, 87-89.

THE CHARTER
of the
CITY OF DETROIT

CHAPTER I.

An Act to Provide a Charter for the City of Detroit, and to repeal all Acts and Parts of Acts in conflict therewith.

INCORPORATION: CITY AND WARD BOUNDARIES

Section 1. The people of the state of Michigan enact: That the inhabitants of the city of Detroit shall continue to be one body politic and corporate, under the name and style of the city of Detroit; and as such shall have, exercise and enjoy such powers of a local legislative and administrative character as are conferred by this act, or by the general laws of the state of Michigan, and shall also exercise and enjoy such implied and incidental powers and rights as are of right possessed by municipal corporations in this state. (As amended by Act approved June 4, 1895.). . . .

Section 2. The powers of local government possessed by said city are divided into two departments, the legislative and administrative. No person or body belonging to one department shall exercise powers properly belonging to the other, except in cases expressly provided in this act. . . .

CHAPTER V.

OFFICERS: THEIR RIGHTS, POWERS AND DUTIES.

Section 1. The mayor shall be the chief executive officer of the city of Detroit, and conservator of its peace. It shall be his duty to keep an office in some convenient place in said city, to be provided by the common council; to see that all officers of said city faithfully comply with and discharge their official duties; to see that all laws pertaining to the municipal government of said city, and all ordinances and resolutuins of the common council be faithfully observed and executed; and he shall have power in his discretion to report to the common council any violations thereof. He shall, from time to time, give the common council such information and recommend such measures as he shall deem necessary or expedient.

Section 2. The mayor shall be paid a salary of five thousand dollars per annum. In case of a vacancy in the office of mayor, or his being unable to perform the duties of the office by reason of sickness, absence from the city, or other cause, the president of the common council shall be acting mayor; and in case, at the same time, there shall be a vacancy in the office of president of the common council, or he shall be unable to perform the duties of his office by reason of sickness, absence from the city, or other cause, the president pro tempore of the common council shall be acting mayor. Such acting mayor shall be vested with all the powers, and shall perform all the duties of mayor until the vacancy or vacancies aforesaid be filled. . . .

CREATION OF THE BOARD OF HEALTH, August 16, 1881 and March 1, 1895

Concern for the problems of health led to the establishment of a Board of Health in 1881. The Board was reorganized in 1895. It was given powers to prevent introduction of contagious diseases as well as to quarantine those who were ill. The Board also had the power to eliminate any nuisances which could cause disease. Prohibitions were also made in regard to limiting the activities of any one who might be carrying a contagious disease.

Source: The Revised Ordinances of the City of Detroit, for the Year 1895. . . . Detroit, 1895, pp. 210-215.

BOARD OF HEALTH

Section 1. The Board of Health shall have power, and it is hereby made their duty:

1. To make diligent inquiry with respect to all nuisances, of every description, in said city, which are, or may be, injurious to the public health, and abate the same.

2. To stop, detain and examine every person coming from a place infected with a pestilential or infectious disease, in order to prevent the introduction of the same into this city.

3. To cause any person, not a resident of this city, who is infected with any infectious or pestilential disease, to be sent back to the place from whence he or she came, or to the pesthouse or hospital.

4. To cause any person, a resident of this city, who is infected with any pestilential or infectious disease, to be removed to the pest-house or hospital, if, in their opinion, the removal of such person is necessary for the preservation of the public health, and can be effected with safety to the patient.

5. To destroy or disinfect, as in their judgment may be deemed proper, any furniture, wearing apparel, goods, wares, or merchandise, or artices or property of any kind, which shall be exposed to, or infected with a contagious or infectious disease: Provided, however, That such property shall be appraised by two disinterested persons, in order that remuneration may be made therefor by the Common Council.

6. To rent proper houses to be used for pest-houses and hospitals, of which they shall have control and

direction, and to employ such nurses, officers, agents, servants or assistants, and provide the necessary furniture, medicines, articles and necessaries for the use of the pest-houses or hospitals, and the persons therein confined, as may be deemed necessary, and when so authorized by the Common Council.

7. To require the occupants of any dwelling house, store, shop or other building in which there shall be any person sick with small-pox, varioloid or other infectious disease, to put up and maintain in a conspicuous place on the front of said dwelling house, store, shop or other building, a card or sign, to be furnished by the Board, on which shall be written or printed, in large letters, the word "Small-Pox," or name of such infectious disease; and in case of the neglect or refusal of any person to comply with such requirements, to remove the patient to the pest-house or hospital.

8. To make and enforce any necessary order compelling any steamboat, or other vessel or craft, having on board any onfected or diseased person or property, not to enter the harbor or remove therefrom.

9. To exercise a general supervision over the health of the city, and to make, from time to time, such recommendations to the Common Council as they deem proper, to promote the cleanliness and salubrity of the city.

10. The said Board shall annually and oftener, if they deem it necessary, divide the city into health districts.

11. The said Board shall provide and keep on hand a supply of cards marked "Small-Pox," to be put upon any house in which there is a person sick of that disease or the varioloid; and such cards, upon application, shall be furnished without charge.

12. Whenever, in their judgment, it shall be necessary for the public health, the said Board may at once take possession of any building, factory, hotel, dwelling-house, outhouse, premises or ground upon which, in their judgment, there exists any nuisance prejudicial to the public health; and if the owner or occupant shall refuse or neglect to forthwith abate such nuisance in the manner directed by said Board, said Board may cause the same to be abated forthwith in such manner as they deem proper, and all expenses incurred shall be a legal claim against the owner and a lien upon the premises, to be collected in the same manner as other special assessments. The said Board may also, when they deem it requisite for the public health, at once, and by force, if necessary, close up such houses, buildings, hotels and premises, and exclude all occupants therefrom until such nuisance shall be fully abated, and the air of such building or premises is throughly purified. Any person who shall resist the action of the Boatd, or their agents under this sub-

division, shall be liable to penalties hereinafter provided.

Sec. 13. Every physician, or person acting as such, who shall have a patient sick of the small-pox, varioloid, or other infectious or pestilential disease, shall forthwith report the fact in writing to the said Board, together with the name and the street, and number of the house where such patient is treated; and every keeper, superintendent or person in charge of any pest-house within the corporate limits of the City of Detroit, or any other pest-house under control of the authorities of said city, to which any person, being a city charge, may be brought sick with infectious or contagious disease, shall at once on the arrival of every such person give notice thereof in writing to the said Board: Provided, That if the person thus brought to such pest-house is a county charge, the notice herein required shall be given also to the County Physician.

Sec. 14. It shall be the duty of any occupants of any dwelling-house, or other building in which there shall be small-pox, varioloid or any infectious disease, to put up and maintain in a conspicuous place on the front of such building, a card or sign, to be furnished by the Board of Health, on which shall be written or printed the word "small-pox" or any infectious disease, and such sign or card shall be kept on such building all the time any person so diseased shall remain therein, and until permission is obtained in writing for the Board of Health to remove the same. . . .

FREDERICK OLMSTED'S RECOMMENDATIONS CONCERNING URBAN IMPROVEMENTS, 1905

Detroit was concerned with the beginnings of urban decay at the turn of the century. As a consequence the Detroit Board of Commerce requested that the early urban planners, Frederick Law Olmsted and Charles Mulford Robinson, make recommendations for improvements. Recognizing the assets of the City, Olmsted made recommendations concerning improvements for the Riverfront area, the parks and the inner city. The selections printed below indicate how the river area and the center of the city might be reconstructed to better serve the needs of the municipality.

Source: Detroit Board of Commerce. Improvement of the City of Detroit; Reports Made by Professor Frederick Law Olsmted, Jr. and Charles Mulford Robinson. Detroit, 1905, pp. 9-13 and 37-43.

I.

Improvement of the River Margin

A The Central Section--the Front

The river margin of Detroit is divided by conditions of use and location into several distinct sections, one of the most important of which is the central one lying between the railroad frontages which border the river east of Brush Street and west of Third Street. This section, pre-eminently THE FRONT OF THE CITY on the river, is mainly appropriated, not only by present use but by the logic of its situation to passenger and local freight business. On account of its central location, opposite the heart of the city where all the main streets and car lines converge, where the financial and office district is permanently centered, and whence the principal retail districts are bound to radiate, no matter in which direction they chiefly grow, this half mile has permanent exclusive advantages for transhipping all the steamboat passengers between Detroit and every point on the vast river and lake system which Detroit commands. The freight of such a locality, though large and certain to grow, is not likely, if we may judge by the experience of seaboard cities, to include a great volume of heavy staples of manufacturing freight, but rather a miscellaneous class of individually small shipments for local distribution.

As the city's inevitable and rapid growth continues, but as time and enterprise develop the enormous possibilities of the summer resort business of the Great Lakes, it will become necessary to carry on upon this limited frontage a volume of business in comparison with which the present lively traffic is a mere trifle. Through the casual, haphazard development of the front by private initiative, facilities have been provided which meet present traffic requirements tolerably well, but in the future it will be necessary to utilize every foot of this space to its maximum capacity, a condition which cannot be met except by intelligent co-operation between all the interested parties. These parties obviously are the steamboat concerns; the merchants and manufacturers who ship and receive freight by the vessels; the passengers who come and go by ferry, excursion and long-distance steamer; the transportation concerns which take care of the freight and passengers on the land side; and finally the city at large, which is dependent for its full prosperity upon the economy, speed, convenience and general satisfaction with which this business is handled.

On account of the vital interest of the city in providing for the upbuilding of this traffic along the most satisfactory lines, and because of certain important incidental benefits which the city might derive from the proper development of the water front, if in planning it account is taken of all public interests instead of only those which would bring direct profit to the transportation companies, it is highly desirable that the city should take the initiative in bringing the various interests into co-operation. . . .

The following project of a possible treatment of The River Front is put forward, not at all as a solution of the problem, because I have only the most superficial acquaintance with the facts, but as a suggestion of the sort of way in which the problem should be approached; namely, with a single eye to meeting in the best possible manner--that is to say, in the way most permanently profitable to the community--the requirements of the various parties which have an interest in the use of the River Front.

Experience everywhere seems to show that the best way of handling such freight is upon a broad, covered wharf or quay, connecting on the water side with the main deck of the steamers and on the land side with the level of the streets used for teaming.

If adequate space can be provided either by getting control of adjacent property on the land side or by building out into the stream, it is possible that it would be an advantage to introduce on the same level a set of tracks equipped with electric flat cars for local transfers of freight from point to point along the quay and between the vessels and the adjacent warehouses. If these tracks should extend to the railroad yards further along the river bank, these electric flat cars would also serve to transfer the ordinary railroad freight cars back and forth for handling material that might be coming or going by railroad, either between the railroad and the steamers or between the railroad and warehouses back of the quay. Such tracks at grade should not, of course, be used for transferring any considerable amount of through freight between the two railroads, and if that necessity should arise a separate provision ought to be made for it, but for local business the direct communication of such tracks at grade with quay and street and warehouse basement would seem highly valuable.

On the other hand, to mix up the passenger business, with all the hurly-burly of freight sheds, any more than can be avoided is extremely inconvenient and undesirable. Even the streets approaching the Front, passing through a wholesale warehouse district and crowded as they will be with heavy teams and rough teamsters, are sure to be an inconvenient and disagreeable means of approach for passengers, as such streets are in every city in the country. The device already employed by some of the steamboat companies of building pavilions for the use of passengers on the roofs of their freight sheds, is an admirable one, and it would seem as though it might be developed by giving means of approach for passengers at this level and providing as far as possible for the waiting rooms, ticket offices, etc., on this upper level, and for landing the passengers here from the upper deck in case of all steamers which can be adapted to the arrangement, so as to care for the passengers independently of the freight business.

Probably, for the immediate future at least, it may be best to confine all the steamboat business (passengers and freight alike) to the main wharf level, and simply provide a continuous open public promenade on the upper deck, which would be reached by steps from the various streets, would connect all the different boat lines in a convenient manner, and would afford at the same time a most valuable public recreation place. This appears to be the present opinion of those steamboat men with whom I have had the opportunity to talk. . . .

HEART OF THE CITY

If to the inevitable and unceasing increase of building space needed to accomodate the development of City, County and Federal business in a great manufacturing center, be added the requirements of museums, theaters, halls for concerts and conventions, and similar quasipublic purposes, a very little thoughtful consideration of the rate of increase in such buildings which accompanies the growth of a modern city in population and wealth will convince anyone who believes in the future of Detroit that even the next generation will erect enough buildings of this class to form a very imposing group, provided that they BE grouped--provided that shapely and convenient spaces be provided for them to face upon so as to bring them into agreeable architectural relationship.

The situation is this: In the region between the City Hall and the County Building lie a certain number of square feet of land distributed in ill-shapen squares and street intersections and occupied by improvements of a certain value, such as paving, parking, monuments and street car tracks; and also a certain number of square feet of building land distributed in more or less irregular lots and occupied by comparatively inexpensive and outworn structures. It is evident that apart from the value invested in these improvements a great deal better results could be secured for all concerned if all this land could only be pooled and then redivided into squares, streets and building land of better shape and better arranged.

The following alternatives seem to confront the city here:

First, the matter may be allowed to drift without change in the street lines, in which case private capital will from time to time replace the present buildings with others of a more costly and permanent sort, the city and various semi-public bodies will purchase lots from time to time at increasing prices and invest large sums of money in new buildings, but the whole region will remain a comparatively ineffective jumble, and the money which is sure to be spent in attempting to beautify both the buildings and the "Squares" will bring a relatively small return.

Second, the city may improve the outlines of the open area by making certain street extensions and widenings, as has been proposed, cutting through many lots, paying practically the full value of every building affected even though but a small piece be taken, and leaving the new frontage occupied in part by ill-shaped remnants of lots which will not afford inducements for the erection of desirable buildings in part by the newly exposed backs and sides of existing buildings, and in part, at the best, by what is to be seen there today, and then the usual process of hap-hazard development will take place, and Detroit will have acquired at large expense shapely squares with a hodge-podge of buildings around them.

Third, the city might make a carefully digested plan for the best utilization of the whole region, and might then acquire under mortgage so much of the property abutting on the present squares as may be necessary in order to give it the power to effect on its own land the desirable changes in street and lot lines and in order to control the needful sites for future public buildings, and it might then take its time and make the actual changes in street lines just so fast as a reasonable regard for the value of present improvements will permit, in the meantime leasing such of the property as need not be vacated at once either to the present occupants or in the open market.

By readjusting the outline between the open space and certain parts of the adjacent building land (thus brought under one control), it should be possible to reach excellent results without a great increase in the total area devoted to streets and squares, whereas if the city does not itself acquire and hold any building land to meet its future needs, it can improve the shape of the open space only by the elimination of so much additional building land--an economic consideration of considerable weight in a region so near the heart of the city.

I would urge, therefore, that the Board of Commerce consider most carefully whether some means cannot be devised for thus controlling, in a large, far-sighted and conservative manner, the future improvement of Cadillac Square and the adjacent building land, so as to get out of it the largest possible returns both direct and indirect. . . .

There is no haste about the realization of this dream. Detroit has all the ages before it, with time and means to accomplish things far beyond our poor conception. I speak of it only to point out that in the treatment of the Campus Martius, of Cadillac Square, of the Grand Circus with its radiating streets and of other problems in this locality it should be borne in mind that time will surely bring forth at the Water Gate some soaring structure that will demand a recognition of unity throughout the heart of the City.

It is for the citizens of Detroit today to see to it that mere lack of deliberate, broad foresight and patient inventive study today shall not compel your successors to throw away and reconstruct the results of your efforts as you must do to some extent to the work of your predecessors if you are to make a success of Cadillac Square.

MUNICIPAL OWNERSHIP OF RAILWAYS, April 7, 1913

Detroit shared many of the problems faced by other growing cities in the twentieth century. Municipal transportation facilities had taken advantage of the boss-ridden corrupt governments by arranging for the best possible conditions in gaining their franchises, as well as paying for them. They were not providing the best possible services for the populous. Consequently, the citizenry decided to have their government take on the responsibility and expenses of managing the street railways. The selection printed from the City Charter indicates the manner of control.

Source: Charter of the City of Detroit. Edition of May 1st, 1925 (Including all Amendments From November 5, 1918 to April 6, 1925). . . Detroit, 1925, pp. 75-76.

Chapter XIII

Street Railway Commission

Municipal Ownership and Operation of Street Railway System

Section 1. The City shall at once proceed to, and as soon as practicable acquire or construct and own, maintain and operate a street railway system beneath, upon and above the surface of the streets of the city and within a distance of ten miles from any portion of its limits that the public convenience may require; and as soon as practicable said system shall be made exclusive. Nothing herein contained shall be construed to prevent the city from making a grant to private parties in relation to said street car system beneath, upon and above said streets.

Commission Created; Appointment; Compensation; Removal:

Sec. 2. There shall be a board to be known as the Board of Street Railway Commissioners, which shall consist of three members, who shall be appointed by the mayor. Said board shall serve without salary and be subject to removal at the will of the mayor.

* * *

Duties of Board:

Sec. 6 It shall be the duty of said board to proceed promptly to purchase, acquire or construct and to own and operate a system of street railways in and for the City, and as soon as practicable to make said system exclusive. Said board shall, whenever it deems it necessary, build extensions and new lines. Such extensions and new lines shall be first approved by the Common Council.

Acquisition of System:

Sec. 7. Said board may purchase or lease, or by appropriate proceedings prescribed by law and in the name of the city condemn all or any part of the existing street railway property in the City, and in like manner said board shall have power to acquire street railway property without the limits of the city as prescribed by law, if the board shall determine, or it may make the necessary purchases of lands, machinery, engines, ties, rails, poles, wires, conduits, cars, tools and all other articles, apparatus, appliances, instruments and things necessary to construct, own, maintain and operate, and said board shall construct, own, maintain and operate, in said city for said city and within a distance of ten miles from any portion of its limits as aforesaid, a system of street railways beneath, upon and above such streets and other places in the city and outside thereof as aforesaid as the common council shall from time to time elect.

NEW CITY CHARTER: INITIATIVE, REFERENDUM AND RECALL, June 25, 1918

Like many other cities in the United States, Detroit's citizens joined the Progressive reform movement by providing means by which they could participate to a greater extent in governmental activities. The provisions for initiative and referendum guaranteed that measures not popular with those in power could be submitted to the citizenry for adoption. The recall provision, which provided for recall of municipal officials, was successfully used in the recall of Mayor Charles Bowles on July 22, 1930.

Source: Charter of the City of Detroit. Adopted by the People of the City of Detroit, June 25, 1918. Filed with the Secretary of State and in Effect June 27, 1918. Detroit, 1918, pp. 5, 25-28, 32-35, 40-41.

PREAMBLE

We, the People of the City of Detroit, desiring to perfect a municipal government which shall more nearly conform to prevailing conditions and meet the growing needs of our city, insure a more efficient system for the administration of its affairs, secure the fullest measure of self-government conferred by the Constitution and laws of the State of Michigan, and promote as far as possible the peace, health, safety and welfare of its people, do ordain and establish this charter.

TITLE I.

INCORPORATION, POWERS, BOUNDARIES AND WARDS

CHAPTER I.

Incorporation and Powers.

Incorporation:

Section 1. The inhabitants of the city of Detroit shall continue to be one body politic and corporate under the name and style of the "City of Detroit," and as such shall have, exercise and enjoy such powers as are conferred by the constitution and laws of the state of Michigan and this charter.

Powers:
Sec. 2. The powers of local government possessed by the city are divided into three departments, the legislative, executive and judicial, and no person or body belonging to one department shall exercise powers properly belonging to another, except in cases especially provided for in this charter.

* * *

CHAPTER II.
INITIATIVE AND REFERENDUM.
Initiative.

Initiatory Petitions:
Section 1. Any proposed ordinance may be submitted to the common council by a petition filed with the city clerk praying that such ordinance be adopted by the council, and that if it be not so adopted, it be submitted to a vote of the electors of the city. Such petition shall be known as an initiative petition. It shall set forth in full the proposed ordinance and shall contain a brief statement of the substance thereof, which statement shall appear on the official ballot as herein provided in the event of the submission of the proposed ordinance to a vote of the electors. The petition shall be signed by qualified electors of the city equal in number to five per cent of the total number of votes cast for all candidates for the office of mayor at the last general municipal election prior to the filing of such petition. Before the circulation of such petition for signature, the proposed ordinance as contained therein shall be submitted to the corporation counsel for approval as to form.

Signatures; Affidavit:
Sec. 2. Each signer of a petition shall sign his name in ink or indelible pencil, and shall place on the petition after his name his place of residence, by street and number, and the date of signature. The signatures to any such petition need not all be appended to one paper, but to each paper constituting a part of such petition there shall be attached an affidavit by the circulator thereof stating the number of signers to such part of the petition, and that each signature appended to the paper is the genuine signature of the person whose name it purports to be, and was made in the presence of the affiant.

Examination by City Clerk:
Sec. 3. Within ten days from the filing of a petition, the city clerk shall ascertain whether it is signed by the required number of qualified electors and shall endorse thereon a certificate of the result of his examination as to its sufficiency.

Supplemental Petitions:

Sec. 4. If the clerk's certificate shows that the number of signatures to the petition is insufficient, an additional paper or papers may be filed at any time within fifteen days from the date of such certificate in the same manner as provided in case of the original petition.

Insufficient Petitions:

Sec. 5. Upon the filing of such additional paper or papers, the clerk shall attach the same to the original petition, and shall within ten days thereafter, examine such additional paper or papers as so attached, and certify the result. If the petition as a whole is still insufficient, or if no additional paper or papers shall have been filed, the clerk shall file the petition in his office and shall notify the council to the effect that a petition has been filed in his office, but that the number of signatures thereto is insufficient, and shall state the substance of the petition, the number of signatures required and the number of signatures attached thereto. The filing of an insufficient petition shall not prejudice the filing of a new petition for the same purpose.

Presentation to Common Council:

Sec. 6. If the certificate of the clerk shows that the petition is sufficient, he shall present the proposed ordinance to the common council at its next regular meeting. The council shall at once proceed to consider the proposed ordinance, and shall take the final action thereon within thirty days from the date of the presentation thereof. If the council fails to adopt the proposed ordinance as presented, or if adopted and the mayor shall veto the ordinance and the council fail to enact it over the mayor's veto, then it shall be submitted to the vote of the electors in the manner herein provided.

Submission of Ordinance:

Sec. 7. Such initiative ordinance shall be submitted at the next regular city or state election held thereafter, or at any primary election, or at any special election called for any purpose, but no special election shall be held solely for the purpose of submitting such proposed ordinance.

Ballots; Vote Required; Taking Effect:

Sec. 8. The ballots used in voting upon such proposed ordinance shall contain the title of the ordinance to be voted on, and a statement of the substance thereof, as contained in the petition, and the two propositions: "For the ordinance" and "against the ordinance." Immediately at the right of each proposition there shall be a square in which by making a cross (X) the voter may vote for or against the proposed ordinance. If a majority of the electors voting on any such proposed ordinance shall vote in favor thereof, it shall thereupon become an ordinance of the city: Provided, that if the subject matter of such ordinance is such as to require more than a majority vote under the constitution or laws of the state, then it shall not go into effect unless it receive such votes as may be so required. The vote on such proposed ordinances shall be taken, counted, returned, canvassed and certified in the same manner as other votes are taken, counted, returned, canvassed and certified at elections held under this charter. Upon the certificate of the board of city canvassers that a proposed ordinance has been adopted as herein provided, the city clerk shall file in his office with the other ordinances of the city the copy thereof as presented to the common council prior to submission. The clerk shall forthwith notify the council of the filing of such ordinance, and the notice thereof shall be entered upon the journal of the council, whereupon such ordinance shall take effect.

Publication; Amendment or Repeal:
Sec. 9. Proposed ordinances for amending or repealing any existing ordinance may be submitted to the council as provided in the preceding sections for initiating other ordinances. Initiated ordinances adopted by the electors shall be published as in the case of other ordinances. Such ordinances shall not be amended or repealed by the council within six months from the date of adoption and thereafter only by a vote of seven members of the council.

Referendum.

Referendum on Ordinances:
Sec. 10. Every ordinance passed by the council, except emergency ordinances as defined in this charter, shall be subject to the referendum, if at any time, before taking effect as herein provided, a petition signed by electors equal in number to ten per cent of the total vote cast for the office of mayor at the last preceding city election at which a mayor was chosen be filed with the city clerk, requesting that such ordinance be repealed by the council or be submitted to the qualified electors for their approval or rejection.

Referendary Petitions:
Sec. 11. The provisions of this chapter relative to the form and manner of signing initiative petitions, the filing, examination, certification and sufficiency thereof, and the presentation thereof to the common council by the city clerk, shall apply to referendary

petitions filed under the provisions hereof.

Suspension of Ordinances:

Sec. 12. If any referendary petition or petitions be filed, as herein provided, and the city clerk shall be unable to make his certificate to the sufficiency or insufficiency thereof within thirty days after the enactment of the ordinance the submission of which to a referendary vote is thereby demanded, such ordinance shall be suspended from taking effect after the expiration of said thirty days and until the date of the certificate of the city clerk as to the sufficiency or insufficiency of such petition or petitions, but not for a longer period than ten days thereafter. If by the certificate of the city clerk such petition or petitions are shown to be sufficient, such ordinance shall not go into effect until it shall be adopted by vote of the electors of the city, as hereinafter provided. If by such certificate, such petition or petitions are certified to be insufficient, such ordinance shall go into effect upon the date of such certificate, if thirty days have elapsed since the approval thereof, or if such period has not elapsed, then at the expiration thereof. No supplemental petitions shall be filed after the expiration of said thirty days. In case more than one referendary petition be filed, all such petitions shall be considered in determining the number of signatures of qualified electors, and shall have the same force and effect as though all the names had been appended to one petition.

Submission of Ordinances:

Sec. 13. Upon the presentation to the council by the city clerk of a referendary petition, the ordinance, the submission of which to a referendary vote is thereby demanded, must be either repealed by the council without delay, or submitted to a vote of the qualified electors of the city for approval or rejection at the next regular city or state election or primary election occurring subsequent to forty days from the date of the presentation of such referendary petition to the council by the city clerk; Provided, That if before such general or primary election, and subsequent to said forty days, a special election shall be held for any other purpose, then such ordinance shall be so submitted at such special election, or, in the discretion of the council, at any special election called for that purpose.

Ballot; Elections; Vote:

Sec. 14. The form of ballot, the manner of conducting elections, and the votes required to adopt any such ordinance shall be the same as herein provided with reference to ordinances initiated by petition.

Notice to Council:
Sec. 15. The city clerk, upon the certificate of the board of city canvassers that an ordinance has been ratified or rejected hereunder, shall notify the common council forthwith. If such ordinance shall have been rejected, it shall upon the filing of such certificate be deemed to have no force or effect.

Uniform Blanks for Petitions:
Sec. 16. Petitions circulated with respect to any proposition shall be uniform in character. The city clerk shall provide and keep on file forms of blanks to be used in the several instances of petitions required by this chapter. . . .

EXECUTIVE DEPARTMENT

Executive or Administrative Powers:
Section 1. The executive or administrative powers of the city, . . . are hereby vested in the mayor, city clerk, and city treasurer. . . and certain officers, boards, and commissions appointed by the mayor. . . .

Discontinuance of Certain Offices:
Sec. 7. Any office hereby authorized, but not specifically named, may at any time be discontinued by the common council, and if there be an incumbent in such office, such discontinuance shall, on notice thereof, discharge him from the office and a further execution of its duties, and his office shall be deemed vacant.

Recall and Removal of Officers:
Sec. 8. Any elective officer provided for in this charter, except judges of courts of record and courts of like jurisdiction, may be recalled by the legal voters of the city or ward in the manner provided by the constitution and laws of this state. Such elective officers and any appointive officers may be removed from office as herein provided.

Resignations:
Sec. 9. Resignations from office shall be made in writing, as follows: By the mayor to the common council, by the councilmen to the president of the common council, by all other elective officers to the mayor, who shall report the same to the council for acceptance, and by all appointive officers to the mayor or other officer or board whose duty it is to fill the vacancy.

Vacancies in Office:
Sec. 10. In the case of expulsion or removal from office, death, resignation, or permanent disability of any officer, his office shall thereby become vacant, and

may be so declared by the common council.

Delivery Over of Books, Papers, Money and Effects:

Sec. 11. Whenever any officer shall resign or be removed from office, or the term for which he shall have been elected or appointed shall expire, he shall, on demand, deliver over to his successor in office all the books, papers, moneys, and effects in his custody as such officer, and in any way appertaining to his office. Every person violating this provision shall be deemed guilty of a misdemeanor, and shall be punished accordingly. Every officer appointed or elected under this charter shall be deemed an officer within the meaning hereof. . . .

RECALL OF MAYOR CHARLES BOWLES, July 22. 1930

After an intense campaign Mayor Bowles was recalled in a special election by the citizens of Detroit. He was charged with tolerating lawlessness, dismissing loyal public servants and mismanaging the city-owned street railway. This campaign began with the signing of a petition for recall by over 100,000 persons. Mr. Bowles had indicated his political ambitions lay far beyond the Mayoralty of Detroit. He hoped to enter state and national politics and even become a Senator some day. The Mayor had replaced an unpopular Police Commissioner with a businessman, Mr. Emmons, who proceeded to raid gambling dens in the absence of the Mayor. When the Police Commissioner was then dismissed for permitting gamblers to operate, rather than the raid as some claimed, the situation became more serious since the Mayor had not admitted the existence of these gamblig establishments. The street railway fares were increased to eight cents which caused a furor, along with charges that gamblers and racketeers were paying for protection. The selections printed below indicate the manner in which the movement for recall proceeded.

Source: "111,270 Sign to Recall Detroit Mayor; Election Must Be Set Within Next 25 Days," New York Times, June 20, 1930.

W. K. Kelsey. "Detroit Rebukes Ambitious Mayor," New York Times, June 29, 1930, III, 2:7.

"Detroit by 30,956, Recalls Mayor Bowles," New York Times, July 23, 1930, 1:4-5.

111,270 Sign to Recall Detroit Mayor; Election Must Be Set Within 25 Days

Detroit, Mich., June 19.--Petitions bearing the names of

111,270 citizens asking the recall of Mayor Bowles were filed today with Richard W. Reading, City Clerk, by Walter B. Cary, leader of the movement, after a conference with political leaders and business men.

The movement began a month ago, following the discharge of Harold H. Emmons as Police Commissioner, and charges that Mayor Bowles had condoned lawlessness.

Only 90,000 signatures were needed under the law, which specifies that the City Clerk, within five days of the filing of petitions, must issue a call for a special election, and the election must be held within twenty days from the latter time.

Mr. Cary this afternoon declared the names presented came from every walk of life and, in effect, were a spontaneous outbreak of public indignation over the way the city affairs have been conducted during the last few months.

Early in the circulation of petitions, persons interested in the Mayor's retention of office had boasted that they would discredit the movement by having fake signatures submitted, with a view to challenging them after the filing.

The recall committee, which had been carefully checking all signatures, took the statement as an added reason for a very careful survey of each petition. As a result, several thousand questionable signatures were thrown aside, and the Prosecuting Attorney was notified of the facts disclosed and asked to take action against any one involved in an action to impose fraudulent signatures on the City Clerk.

Meanwhile, Mayor Bowles was in conference with Louis J. Colombo, attorney, and it was reported that the Mayor contemplated manamus proceedings in an effort to halt the recall election. Clarence E. Wilcox, Corporation Counsel, previously had requested that he be notified when the petitions were filed, indicated that he might be interested in the court action.

DETROIT REBUKES AMBITIOUS MAYOR

Detroit, June 26.--Because more than 100,000 qualified electors have signed petitions for the recall of Mayor Charles Bowles, Detroit has given the country an impression of serious trouble in her municipal affairs. Such an idea is far from correct. The municipal departments are functioning well. A good many people are disappointed in Mayor Bowles, and others believe in his sinister intentions, but there have been no explicit charges of misfeasance, malfeasance or graft.

Mayor Bowles, when he resigned what is practically a life job as criminal court judge to run for Mayor, said he took the chance because he was ambitious. After the Mayoralty, the Governorship of Michigan; then a Senatorship; then--no one but himself can say how far the Bowles imagination ran. But one who aspires so high must have something more than ambition: at least, that is true in Detroit. And except for ambition, Mayor Bowles is held to have shown few assets to entitle him to preferment, or even to keep his job.

Detroit a Proud City

Detroit believes herself politically better than most cities. This is because for many years Detroit has run her affairs without interference. A generation ago the Legislature passed a bill, largely a Detroit creation, giving Michigan cities the widest possible power of home rule. Under the act Detroit adopted a new charter which gave her a Mayor and a Council of nine, nominated and elected without regard to party. From that time on, the city has had a good Council, as Councils go (at least a responsive one); and it has had efficient Mayors and one or two who, if they were not brilliant, at least wrought no harm.

Mayor Bowles won in last November's election because his opponents had both been Mayors and had both failed to fulfill Detroit's idea of what a Mayor should be, an idea which, since the administrations of James Couzens, has been high. The voters, selecting between two failures and an unknown, chose the unknown.

The ambitious Mayor Bowles proceeded to reveal himself. He appointed as Commissioner of Public Works a politician of the old school, John Gillespie. Under the party system Mr. Gillespie had succeeded in making two Mayors, one of whom promptly unmade himself, either with or against Mr. Gillespie's advice, while the other had to rid himself of Mr. Gillespie to save his own career. Seeing Mr. Gillespie heading a department and making himself the Mayor's chief adviser, the electorate began to think long thoughts. These thoughts became very serious when Mayor Bowles made other appointments indicating he intended, with Mr. Gillespie's aid, to build a political machine in the City Hall.

Mayor's First Mistake

Before putting himself in Mr. Gillespie's hands, however, Mayor Bowles had blundered by replacing an unpopular Police Commissioner with a lawyer and business man of standing. That blunder was made manifest in a peculiar way. The newspapers discovered a number of handbooks and gambling places operating openly and apparently with official toleration. One was visible from the windows of Bowles' office, yet the Mayor declined to believe it existed. When Mayor Bowles went to Louisville to watch the Kentucky Derby, Commissioner Emmons started to raid the gambling dens. On his return the Mayor angrily discharged Mr. Emmons, not, he said, for raiding the gamblers, but for permitting them to operate. Mr. Emmons retorted that Mayor Bowles had himself named the commander of the vice squad, the official whose duty it was to prevent gambling.

Such mistakes made an executive ridiculous even in the eyes of his friends, still more so to those who have watched impartially and withheld judgment. There were plenty of the latter.

Outcome in Doubt

Now it must be conceded that in six months of public office Mayor Bowles has done little harm to Detroit, however ridiculous he may have made himself in the eyes of the people. So far as any one knows, the municipal departments are functioning with their ususal efficiency. But Detroit is peculiar. For one thing, it is a young man's city, and while young men may be themselves foolish, they do not tolerate even the appearance of foolishness in their rulers. Then, lack of party control, together with civil service in all the departments but one, has made the construction of a strong political machine almost impossible.

Mayor Bowles may not be recalled, and if he is, he may be re-elected. If the recall succeeds, an election must be held within thirty days, and Mr. Bowle's name goes on the ballot automatically. So far there is not a sign of a candidate to oppose him. But recalled or not, Mayor Bowles has had his lesson.

Detroit by 30,956, Recalls Mayor Bowles

DETROIT, July 22.--Mayor Charles Bowles has been "recalled" by the voters of this city, the largest that ever undertook to rid itself of a chief executive by this method.

In a total vote of 210,770 a majority of 30,956 was cast in favor of the recall.

The vote of the 852 precincts of the city was: For recall, 120,863; against, 89,907.

Admission of the Mayor's defeat was made soon after 10 o'clock tonight, when the count of 550 precincts showed that the supporters of the recall had already rolled up a 22,000 vote lead with 300 more precincts to come.

A heavy vote was cast in all parts of the city and much of it in the early part of the day. The northwesterm and western section, where Mayor Bowles rolled up a big lead in the election of last Fall, polled a large vote and gave encouragement to the Mayor's friends, but this soon faded when the actual figures of the polling came in.

Indications were seen that the women of the city did not vote as heavily as they did in the last election. In some precincts the percentage was only 20 per cent for the fair sex.

As a result of today's decision, another election for Mayor must be held within thirty days. It is expected that Mayor Bowles will again be a candidate for the place which he won in November by a majority of about 8,500 votes. This will be his third candidacy.

The twelve-day campaign against the Mayor has been bitter. His recall was asked on charges that he had tolerated lawlessness, dismissed faithful public servants and mismanaged the municipally owned railway.

Detroit Riot, June 21, 1943

Racial tensions rose to a feverish pitch in the city in 1943, in the midst of the war effort. A riot of such intensity broke out that Federal troops were sent in by President Franklin D. Roosevelt. Twenty-three citizens were killed, and a curfew was established between 10 P. M. and 6 A. M. Only workers were exempted. Michigan Governor Harry F. Kelly imposed martial law in Detroit and its environs. The Federal troops were eventually able to establish order as Negro leaders cooperated with them.

Source: "23 Dead in Detroit Rioting; Federal Troops Enter City on the Orders of Roosevelt," New York Times, June 22, 1943, 1:1 and 7:3-6.

Detroit, June 21

Federal troops in full battle regalia, with jeeps, trucks and armored cars, moved into Detroit tonight to help city police, home guards and State troops restore order in the country's worst race riots since the East St. Louis (Ill.) distrubances in the first World War.

/After Federal troops arrived and President Roosevelt's proclamation calling for peace had been received, rioters dispersed and quiet was restored, according to the Associated Press. Mayor Edward J. Jeffries stated at midnight that the situation was much improved./

The death toll at 10:20 P.M. had reached twenty-three, including twenty Negroes and three white persons. The injured, overflowing hospitals, numbered at least 600 and the number arrested and taken to jails and prisons exceeded that number.

With Detroit and its metropolitan-area population of about 2,500,000 persons--tens of thousands of them employed in Dteroit's many war factories--under a state of emergency, Federal troops came from Fort Wayne, Ind., and Mt. Clemens, Mich., near Detroit.

They augmented two batallions of military police from Fort Custer and River Rouge Park as the shootings, beatings and pillaging continued abated.

The Hour Battle With Snipers

Late tonight local and State police pumped more than 1,000 rounds of ammunition and dozens of tear gas bombs into an apartment house to rout Negroes sniping from upper windows.

The siege had begun at 9:15 P. M., a few minutes after several Negroes were seen to run into the building with shotguns and revolvers.

The police first used the tear gas, which drove out most of the tenants on the lower floors, but the besieged group held out.

The police began to return fire with fire and the neighborhood rang with shots for more than two hours, the battle ending with the surrender of the Negroes. Two of them had been killed and a policeman, Lawrence Adams, was wounded seriously.

The Federal troops did not take part in the apartment house siege, but assisted other police in patrolling the riot areas, mostly in the downtown Negro section.

The Federal soldiers rode down Woodward Avenue. Detroit's major thoroughfare. They had orders to "clear the streets." With 1,110 assigned here, 1,200 others were held in reserve at Fort Wayne.

Only Workers Escape Curfew

All persons, except those going to and from their jobs in war plants, already had been ordered to stay in their homes under the 10 P. M. to 6 A. M. curfew ordered by Gov. Harry F. Kelly when he declared that a state of emergency existed.

Brig. Gen. William E. Guthner, in charge of military police for the Army's Sixth Service Command, announced that he had been authorized by his headquarters at Chicago to "cooperate with State and city police."

General Guthner said the request for Federal troops was made by Governor Kelly after the mobs had been ignored his emergency proclamation. It was learned that 2,000 additional troops would arrive in Detroit tomorrow.

Shootings, stabbings and hundreds of street fights throughout the metropolitan area had led Governor Kelly to declare the state of emergency.

Detroit's municipally owned Receiving Hospital, whose chief surgeon, Dr. Austin E. Howard, described the riots "as the worst calamity in Detroit's history," overflowed with injured. It was necessary to borrow blood plasma from the Red Cross to treat seriously injured victims.

Of the dead, twelve succumbed at Receiving Hospitals. Others died in ambulance en route to the Hospitals, and several were found dead in the streets. One white man was found shot to death in the Negro section and a Negro was found dead in a theatre with six bullet wounds. The injured included a police man who had been shot six times.

Three Counties Under Curbs

Detroit, June 21--Governor Harry F. Kelly tonight imposed his modified form of martial law on three southwestern Michigan counties, comprising the Detroit metropolitan area.

In addition, Governor Kelly ordered the curfew also in the three counties, Wayne, Oakland, and Macomb.

All motion-picture houses, theatres and other places of amusement were ordered closed until further orders, and the sale of all alcoholic beverages was indefinitely suspended.

Gatherings and assemblages were forbidden under a separate proclamation issued by Governor Kelly and all persons were banned carrying firearms except the police and the military.

Governor Kelly was called to Detroit by Mayor Edward J. Jeffries shortly before noon today, when Mayor Jeffries admitted the situation was out of hand. Governor Kelly was attending a conference of Governors at Columbus, Ohio.

Troops Ordered Mobilized

Before flying to Detroit in an army plane Mr. Kelly telephoned Brig. Gen. LeRoy C. Pearson, State Adjutant General, in Lansing, ordered him to mobilize the 6,000 Michigan State troops. He also ordered Michigan State police, to the number of 500, moved into Detroit.

Later in the afternoon the State troops, except for those in the Upper Peninsula, were ordered to Detroit and began arriving early this evening.

Governor Kelly and Mayor Jeffries conferred earlier with military officials, and while no specific request was made then for Federal troops the military police battalion stationed here was put on the alert, and a second battalion was ordered in from Fort Custer.

Auxiliary police were mobilized at noon to help out the regular 3,500 members of the Detroit police, most of whom had been on duty since early this morning. It was estimated that all city and State police and State troops on duty in Detroit tonight numbered close to 6,000 men with more due to arrive Tuesday.

The Governor's Proclamation

The text of Governor Kelly's proclamation was as follows:

"I, Harry F. Kelly, Governor of the State of Michigan and Commander in Chief of the military forces of the said State of Michigan, hereby declare a state of emergency and the necessity for the armed forces of the State of Michigan to aid and assist, but in subordination thereto, all duly constituted civil authorities in the execution of the law of the State.

"The necessity for such aid and assistance is declared to extend to the following counties of the State of Michigan, namely: Wayne, Oakland and Macomb.

"In witness whereof, I have hereunto set my hand and caused to be affixed the great seal of the State of Michigan this twenty-first day of June, 1943."

* * *

Governor, Mayor in Radio Pleas

At 6:30 o'clock both Governor Kelly and Mayor Jeffries went on the air with a plea for observance of the law and asking people to remain off the streets.

Most downtown Detroit stores were closed early this afternoon at Mayor Jeffries' request. Ordinarily Detroit stores remain open until 9 P. M. on Mondays.

Street car service was stopped in several sections of the city where the trouble was most acute.

At 8 P. M. a crowd of more than 500 persons gathered in front of the City Hall and in front of the Postoffice. Buses were stopped, trolleys were pulled off their wires and squads of police were rushed to the scene. Several people were arrested before the crowd was dispersed.

* * *

The rioting began about 10:45 P. M. Sunday, apparently with a fight between a Negro and a white man on Belle Isle Bridge, when large crowds were leaving the island.

The fighting became general as rumors spread through the excited crowds and, as police and sailors from the near-by naval armory cleared the bridge, trouble began out on Belle Isle itself and in Gabriel Richard Park off the mainland side of the bridge.

During the night the rioting spread through the near east and north sides of the city, with both white and Negro crowds roaming the streets.

Workers attempting to go to their jobs this morning were attacked and many of them were injured.

Police received reports in the morning that bands of men had looted pawnshops in Negro districts and had stollen guns and ammunition. All pawnshops and hardware stores were ordered to lock up firearms.

After twelve hours of rioting injured patients were still arriving at the receiving hospital at the rate of one each two minutes. Surgeons said that some of them, apparently still under the influence of hysteria, attempted to knife or injure the doctors and nurses attending them.

* * *

POST-WAR IMPROVEMENT PLANS, 1944

The government of the city of Detroit, as did many other municipal administrations, appointed a committee to make plans for post-war changes which would improve the living and working conditions. In addition provisions had to be made for necessary construction, which had been postponed during the depression and war. Finally, the Committee attempted to develop arrangements for the returning servicemen who would not be able to find positions in the private economic sector. Plans were made to construct a new civic center, including municipal offices, new expressways, a new airport, enlargement of Wayne University, creation of the Wayne University Medical Center to provide necessary health services for the city, new recreational facilities and additional public housing.

Source: Detroit Postwar Improvement Committee. Your Detroit, A Finer City in Which to Live and Work. . . . Detroit, 1944.

Three Objectives of the Public Program for a Finer Detroit

1

To Provide Additional Facilities Designed to Make Our City a Finer Place in Which to Live and Work.

First objective of our post-war public improvement program is to bring our city's present facilities up to date. As the City has aged, buildings and equipment have become antiquated, totally inadequate or worn out and should be renovated or replaced. Many new structures and facilities are necessary if we are to improve the living and working conditions of the entire community. Such programs are provided for by the public improvement program.

2

To Catch Up on the Needed Public Construction Which We Postponed During the Depression and the War.

The SECOND objective of this program is to carry on with public improvements from where we left off in the early thirties. Since then very little has been spent on new construction or new equipment. Meanwhile, however, both the population and the built-up areas of our city have been expanding at an amazing rate. This great expansion makes doubly necessary many new facilities immediately after the War. . . schools, play grounds, parks, sewers, paved streets and alleys, and other public structures.

Your city government recognizes its responsibilities and its opportunities: provision therefore has been made in the public improvement program to make up for the years of inadequate construction.

3

To Provide Worthwhile Employment For Our Returning Servicemen and War Workers During the Period of Industrial Reconversion to Peacetime Production if Necessary.

About 160,000 Detroiters are now in the armed forces. Many of these men and women will return to our city, although probably not at one time. Many will find private employment and some will return to schools and colleges. But for many others the public improvement program could provide useful work during the period of reconversion to peacetime production.

About 375,000 workers in excess of previous maximum employment are now working in Detroit. After the war, many will leave Detroit, some will go back to school, and many women will return to their homes. For a large number of those needing employment, the public improvement program could provide work during the period of readjustment.

A New Civic Center

Your city administrative offices are now scattered throughout more than twenty separate buildings, most of which are located at some distance from each other. If, when doing business with the city, you have had to travel from one office to another to complete your transaction, you will realize the inconvenience of this arrangement. Bringing most of these offices together at a central, readily accessible point would facilitate more orderly inter-relationship between departments. Consequently, economy of operation is an important consideration of centralization.

To remedy the present condition, the Common Council has approved the development of a Civic Center on the Detroit River at the foot of Woodward Avenue. Preliminary studies of the initial writs are now underway.

The estimated cost of these units is $25,000,000.

* * *

New Expressways

Of all the various projects now under construction, perhaps none is of greater importance to Detroiters than the proposed system of expressways, wider and straighter streets, and the elimination of traffic bottlenecks. Detroit, center of the automotive industry, has been and no doubt will continue to be a city where private transportation is paramount.

* * *

Our New Air Gateway

Our present airport has long since ceased to serve adequately those of us who use air transportation, air express, or air mail. After the war, many more of us will take to the air, either as passengers on commercial airlines or in our own airplanes. Additional studies are now being made of new sites and plans are moving forward for the development of the new airport. . . which will cost $6,650,000, exclusive of land cost. Included in the development is a terminal building, which will meet the initial requirements of a first-class airport.

Wayne University

Wayne University is destined to become one of the nation's great educational centers. Even today, despite its wholly inadequate quarters and facilities, it is truly a people's university, where Detroiters may gain knowledge and training for civic service, industry, medicine, the arts, and many other pursuits necessary to urban living. An expanded Wayne University will bring to us and our children added opportunities for earning a livelihood and for the enjoyment of the richer life which knowledge affords.

* * *

Wayne University Medical Center

As a contribution to the health of the whole community, it is important that Detroit should have a completely up-to-date medical center such as that now being planned for Wayne University. With almost a quarter of our entire population working in industry, it is also important that Detroit should have specialized facilities to care for industrial accidents and diseases.

The Common Council has allocated a half million dollars for the site of the medical center. . . .

New Places to Play

Our children need more places to play in every neighborhood. Many areas, which have been built up solidly with apartments and flats, should have special playlots that will take children off the streets by giving them suitable places to play in sunlight and fresh air. Older children need protected spaces large enough for baseball, lawn games, tennis, soccer, and other organized games.

To overcome this deficiency, the public improvement program provides for improving sixteen parks and playgrounds at a cost of $6,000,000 and the development of several sites acquired in recent years.

* * *

Permanent Public Housing for Thriving Communities

The construction of permanent public housing was interrupted by the war. The public improvement program will carry on this important work. Sites have already been acquired for two of these projects in the inner east and west side areas. Hundreds of run-down, unsanitary dwellings will be replaced by modern structures, amidst cheap, airy environments. The two projects will provide 2,200 family units.

* * *

BLIGHT ELIMINATION IN DETROIT, 1946

Recognizing the necessity for swift action after the Second World War the Housing Commission faced the problem of inner city deterioration. The means of avoiding complete economic decline had to be determined. The Commission recognized that either the solution of public housing or that of complete private development would not answer the total needs of the inner city. Mayor Edward Jeffries proposed a program of cooperation between the public and private sectors. This joint effort would provide better working and living conditions.

Source: Detroit Housing Commission. The Detroit Plan; A Program for Blight Elimination. Detroit, 1946.

Detroit, like other major cities of the nation, is faced with the problem of decay at its heart.

We present here the Detroit plan for solution of this problem of urban blight. Our plan is not suggested as the final or perfect answer but as a suggestion which we hope will be improved upon by work in other cities.

To the initiated in the problems of a metropolitan area. the story of blight needs no explanation. All are familiar with basic characteristics: the decline of property values. the flight of old residents, the increased ratio between tenants and home owners, and the growth of slums.

The results are equally obvious. In Detroit as in other cities, schools and other public installations have been left only partly used by the flight of the residents to new neighborhoods. As contributions from the blight area to the general financial support of the city have decreased, area obligations for police, fire and health protection have become an increasing drain upon the city treasury. In Detroit, as in most cities, the blight has particularly struck areas immediately surrounding the high-value downtown commercial district, and has led to speculation as to whether this district, so essential to the general welfare of the city can be maintained surrounded by an ever increasing zone of slum and poverty.

Detroit, like other cities, sought the basic causes and possible basic remedies. It was suggested initially that the slum area could best be cleared and the slum districts resettled through erection of project housing by the Federal Public Housing Authority. Immediate objections became apparent.

It was suggested, with considerable reason, that sole dependence upon public housing to turn back the blight progression could only lead ultimately to an entire city of subsidized housing. It was further pointed out that surrounding the central commercial district with an increasing number of inhabitants of subsidized housing would not be conducive to the maintenance of that district. Attention was given to the possibility of redeveloping and resettling the area through private investment. The immediate obstacle in Detroit was identical to that met by other cities with the same thought. Acquired developed land, even though the housing upon it is of a slum type, leads to an acquisition cost beyond the capabilities of either the speculative or investment builder. . . . Detroit therefore approached the problem of how to provide for private enterprise building sites within the budget of the private builder. This led to the program now known as the "Detroit Plan."

The Detroit Plan was initially conceived by Mayor Edward J. Jeffries and given to the Detroit Housing Commission, a public housing authority with city developmental status, for development. . . .

The study between city and cooperating heads of the private construction industry resulted in this plan to clear slums on a basis whereby the City of Detroit will take an initial loss on land acquisition and preparation and later recover that loss through increased tax revenues from the redeveloped site.

The close cooperation between the private builder and the city official is. . .essential to the plan. Detroit, like other cities, has experienced in the past efforts by each group to do the job alone--all led to failure. Planning entirely from the City Hall or Washington inevitably led to criticism that it was an "ivory tower" program not affected by practicalness. Similarly, when private builders have submitted their own plans for redevelopment of slum areas they have almost invariably led to governmental criticism that too much public money is being sought for a profit-making individual.

* * *

In the history of Detroit, public housing has been the only organization to do a constructive job of slum clearance. This program, of course, has been woefully inadequate. Private enterprise has maintained that they could and would perform the major part of our slum clearance job if given the proper sort of cooperation. This proposed program should serve as an invitation to private capital to proceed.

WALTER REUTHER'S PROPOSAL FOR URBAN REDEVELOPMENT, December 8, 1956

The president of the United Auto Workers, Walter P. Reuther, indicated his own personal concern, as well as those of his union members who lived and worked in Detroit, over the continuing decay of the inner city. He proposed formation of a municipal redevelopment corporation to help reconstruct the urban slum area. This organization would work with the City Plan Commission and other agencies to rebuild the area.

Source: "Reuther Presses Detroit on Slums," New York Times, December 9, 1956, 139:3.

Walter P. Reuther proposed today that a municipal redevelopment corporation be formed here to rehabilitate the city's industrial slums.

In a letter to Mayor Albert E. Cobo and Detroit's Common Council, the president of the United Automobile Workers said his union would contribute $10,000 immediately as "seed money" to get such a corporation started.

He suggested that the industrial redevelopment unit work along the same lines as the Citizens Redevelopment Corporation of Detroit, which already has initiated a major residential project in a previously blighted area near the city's downtown business center.

Mr. Reuther commended the City Council for taking the initiative in October in seeking Federal aid aimed at bringing into useful production land now occupied by idle and obsolete industrial plants.

"If this land were cleared," Mr. Reuther said, "there would be ample room within the city for modern, clean, and technologically advanced plants that could produce a variety of products and add to the gross product of the city."

The availability of such plants, he said, could take up the slack in the city's economy created by the abandonment of existing plants and by the exodus into the suburbs of companies still in business.

New plants within the city would also have conveniently available a large source of trained workers, he said. Many such workers, he added, have been stranded and left jobless by the collapse of long-established companies formerly employing large numbers in Detroit.

As a first step toward industrial redevelopment of the city, Mr. Reuther suggested that Mayor Cobo and the

Council call a special citizens' meeting to set up a board and representative community industrial rehabilitation committee. He proposed that this committee work with the City Plan Commission and other appropriate municipal agencies to analyze the problem and then work out a program to meet it, including methods of financing from both private and public sources.

Finally, he said, the committee should take steps to create a non-profit industrial rehabilitation corporation that would serve as the instrument for raising funds and securing the necessary loans to finance the redevelopment of carefully selected industrial sites.

The Citizens Redevelopment Corporation, now at work in the residential field, was formed in 1955 and subsequently raised $400,000 through contributions.

This group and a private Chicago developer have begun a $26,000,000 undertaking that aims to transfer fifty-three acres of barren slum-cleared property into a flowering residential community. Ground was broken on Oct. 16 for the first unit of this project, a twenty-two story apartment tower expected to cost about $3,350,000.

100 MILLION DOLLAR RIVERFRONT CENTER, March, 1959

Detroit continued to plan the redevelopment of her downtown and riverfront area. As the municipal government had decided during the war to have joint responsibility with private enterprise, the private sector was now taking on its responsibility recognizing that this was the best means of preserving the commercial aspects of the downtown area. This part of the total urban redevelopment program was important for the inner city.

Source: John M. Carlisle. "New $100 Million Riverfront Center." Detroit News, March 20, 1959, pp. 1-2.

Plans for a $100 million downtown development west of the Civic Center were announced today by Karl H. Smith president of the Detroit real estate firm of Smith-Bisschop & Co.

It will be the largest single development of its kind in Detroit history.

* * *

Smith said he and his associates plan to build:

•A hotel with more than 30 stories and 1,500 rooms, using "a new design where every room is an outside room."

•Three 12-story luxury apartment houses, complete with swimming pools.

•An automotive and industrial exhibits building and a merchandise mart for permanent displays.

•A shopping center, a restaurant, traffic-free covered pedestrian malls and underground parking facilities.

Smith said the first work will start within six months and said the entire project should be completed within three years.

The site covers 23 acres, all of it now owned by three railroads. . . . It is between Fort Street and the Detroit River, and the Civic Center and the site of a new $23 million post office at Fort and Eighth.

Smith said the three apartment houses will be built first. The schedule for the rest of the construction will depend upon how long it takes the railroads to relocate their facilities, and on obtaining the necessary financing. . . .

The area at Third and the Detroit River will be the site of the three apartment buildings, . . .

BIBLIOGRAPHY

The works cited have been carefully selected to indicate the major sources to be consulted for further research on the growth and development of Detroit. Materials listed have been published during the nineteenth and twentieth centuries. The variety of works were chosen to provide a cross-section of the information on the social, economic and political life of the city. Students should also consult Reader's Guide to Periodical Literature, and Social Science and Humanities Index for further articles on Detroit.

PRIMARY SOURCES

The Automotive History Collection of the Detroit Public Library; A Simplified Guide to Its Holdings. Boston, 1966, 2 vols.

Bureau of Governmental Research, Detroit. Arguments for and Against the City Manager Plan for Detroit; Submitted at the Request of the Detroit Board of Commerce, By the Detroit Bureau of Governmental Research. Detroit, 1927.

--. A Quarter-Century of Citizen Concern With Government; A Preface and a Bibliography of the Detroit Bureau of Governmental Research, 1916-1941. Detroit, 1941.

Burton, M. Agnes, ed. Governor and Judges Journal. Proceedings of the Land Board of Detroit. Detroit, 1915.

The Centennial Celebration of the Evacuation of Detroit by the British, July 11, 1796-July 11, 1896. Report of the Proceedings, With the Addresses. . . comp. by C, M, Burton. Detroit, 1896.

The Charter of the City of Detroit with Amendments Thereto and the Acts of the Legislature Relating to or Affecting the City of Detroit. comp. Timothy E. Torsney. . . Detroit, 1904.

The Charter of the City of Detroit and Several Acts of the Legislature Relating to the Several Boards, Commissions, the Courts of the City. . . with the General Election Laws. comp. John H. Smeed. Detroit, 1893.

Charter of the City of Detroit. Adopted. . . June 25,

1918. In Effect June 27, 1918. Detroit, 1918.

Charter of the City of Detroit. Edition of May 1st, 1925 (Including all Amendments from November 5, 1918, to April 6, 1925). . . Detroit, 1925.

Charter of the City of Detroit; Revised to January 1, 1935. . . Detroit, 1935.

City Health. August 10 - date. Detroit, 1910 - date.

The Compiled Ordinances of the City of Detroit of 1904. Detroit, 1904.

The Compiled Ordinances of the City of Detroit of 1920. Detroit, 1920.

The Compiled Ordinances of the City of Detroit of 1926. Detroit, 1926.

Corporation of the Town of Detroit. Act of Incorporation and Journal of the Board of Trustees, 1802-1805. Detroit, 1922.

Croghan, George. George Croghan's Journal of His Trip to Detroit in 1767, With His Correspondence Relating Thereto. . . . Ann Arbor, 1939.

Detroit. Assessors Board. Annual Report. Land Valuation Maps of Detroit. . . Showing Unit-foot Land Values. . . As Adopted by the Board of Assessors and Confirmed by the Board of Review. 1926 - date. Detroit, 1926 - date.

Detroit. Auditor General. . . . Annual Report. 1st - date. 1937/38 - date. Detroit, 1938 - date.

Detroit Board of Commerce. Detroit's Industrial Advantages. Detroit, 1905.

------------------------. . . . Labor and the Detroiter. Detroit, 1939.

------------------------. Improvement of the City of Detroit; Reports Made by Professor Frederick Law Olmsted, jr. and Mulford Robinson. Detroit, 1905.

Detroit Board of Trade. Statistical Tables of the Detroit Board of Trade for the Year 1882, With the Act of Incorporation, Constitution, By-laws, Rules, Standards and Lists of Members and Officers. . . . comp. John K. Maciver. Detroit, 1883.

Detroit. Budget Bureau. Appropriation for the Maintenance of the Government of the City of Detroit. 1896/97 - date. Detroit, 1897 - date. 1896/97 - 1926/27 issued by the Controller's Office. 1927/28 - date issued by the Budget Bureau.

----------------------. Capital Improvement Six Year and Reserve Program . . . Report. 1942/48. 1942/48 - 1944/50 issued by the Capital Improvement Program Committee. 1950/56 - date by the Postwar Improvement Committee.

Detroit Citizens League. Petition for Election Commission: Charter Amendment. Detroit, 1916.

Detroit. City Engineer's Office. Detroit River Front. A Report for the Mayor and the Mayor's Port Commission. November, 1928. Perry A. Fellows, City Engineer. Detroit, 1928.

Detroit. City Plan Commission. Annual Report. 1924 - date. Detroit, 1925 - date. 1943 - date have Title: Planning Detroit. . . . Annual Report.

------------------------------. . . . Detroit Master Plan. Detroit, 1951.

------------------------------. . . . Economic Base of Detroit. Detroit, 1944.

------------------------------. . . . Master Plan Report. No. 1-7. Detroit, 1946-48.

------------------------------. The People of Detroit. City Plan Commission. City of Detroit. . . Detroit, 1946.

------------------------------. Present Land Use in Detroit. A Master Plan Report. Detroit, 1946.

------------------------------. An Urban Redevelopment Project in Detroit. Rebuilding Deteriorated Areas of the City. . . .

Detroit Civil Service Commission. Annual Report. No. 1 - date. 1913 - date. Detroit, 1914 - date.

--------------------------------. Rules of the Civil Service Commission, City of Detroit. September 1, 1942. Detroit, 1942. See also Rules. . . . 1944 and later.

Detroit. Commission on Children and Youth. Report.

1953 - date. Detroit, 1953 - date.

Detroit. Commission on Community Relations. Report. 1953 - date. Detroit, 1953 - date.

Detroit. Common Council. Journal. 1802-/05 - date. Detroit, 1815 - date. 1815-24 has title: Proceedings of the Board of Trustees.

Detroit. Controller's Office. Annual Report. 1862/63 - 1920/21. Detroit, 1863 - 1921.

------------------------------. Report on the Finances of the City of Detroit, Michigan. 1935 - Present. Detroit, 1935 - Present.

Detroit. Department of Public Works. Annual Report. 1902/03 - date. Detroit, 1903 - date.

Detroit. Education Board. Annual Report. 1869 - date. Title varies: 1869 - 1935/36, Annual Report; 1938/39 - date, The Superintendent's Annual Report.

------------------------. Journal of Proceedings. 1895/96 - date. Detroit, 1896 - date.

The Detroit Educational Bulletin. 1917/18 - date. Detroit, 1918 - date.

Detroit Health Department. Annual Report. 1-35. Detroit, 1882 - 1915/16.

Detroit. Housing Commission. . . . Annual Report, 1933/35 - date. Detroit, 1935 - date.

----------------------------. The Detroit Plan; A Program for Blight Elimination. Detroit, 1946.

----------------------------. A Decade of Public Service. Public Housing or Slums; A Brief Account of Ten Years of Public Housing in Detroit. Detroit, 1948.

Detroit Illustrated. The Commercial Metropolis of Michigan. . . . Detroit, 1891.

Detroit. Mayor. Annual Message. 1824 - date. Detroit, 1825 - date.

Detroit Metropolitan Regional Planning Commission. Report. 1948/49 - date. Detroit, 1949 - date.

Detroit Metropolitan Area Traffic Study. Report. J. B.

Carroll, director. Detroit, 1955.

Detroit, Parks and Boulevards. Report. 1889 - Present. Detroit, 1889 - present.

Detroit. Police Department. Annual Report, 1st - date. 1865/66 - date. Detroit, 1866 - date. Before 1931 most years are also included in Detroit. Annual Report. 1916/17 has title: Study of the Detroit Police Department. 1958 - present has title: Annual Report, Annual Statistical Report.

Detroit. Postwar Improvement Committee. Your Detroit, A Finer City in Which to Live and Work. . . . Detroit, 1944.

Detroit Public Library. Municipal Charters. Selected List. 1913. Detroit, 1913

Detroit. Public Lighting Commission. Annual Report. Nos. 1-23. 1895/96 - 1917/18. Detroit, 1896 - 1918. No longer separately published. Now compiled in report by City Controller.

Detroit Public Welfare Department. . . . Annual Report. 1908/09 - date. Detroit, 1909 - date.

--------------------------------. . . . Monthly Statistics. 1945 - date. Detroit, 1945 - date. Title from 1950 - date: Welfare Progress and Problems.

Detroit. Rapid Transit Commission. Rapid Transit Plan for Metropolitan Detroit with a Suggested Plan for Financing Expressways and Rapid Transit, 1949. Detroit, 1949.

Detroit. Recreation Department. Report. No. 1 - date, 1915 - date. Detroit, 1915 - date.

Detroit Street Railways Department. . . . Annual Report. No. 1 - date. 1922/23 - date. Detroit, 1923 - date. 1925/26 has title: Report of the Auditor [and] Annual Report. 1939/40 - not published.

Detroit Treasurer's Office. Annual Report of the City Treasurer. 1898/9 - 1915/16. Detroit, 1899 - 1916. Ceased publication.

Detroit Water Supply Department. Annual Report. No. 1- date, 1852 - date. Detroit, 1853 - date.

Detroit Stock Exchange, 1907-1931. Detroit, 1931.

Documents Relating to Detroit and Vicinity, 1805-1813, in Michigan Historical Collections, vol. 40, 1929, pps. 1-754.

Doxiadis, Constantinos A. Emergence and Growth of an Urban Region: The Developing Urban Detroit Area. Detroit, 1966-1970. 3 vols.

Farmer, Silas, et. al. Map and Manual of the City of Detroit. Detroit, 1872.

Great Lakes - St. Lawrence Association. Special Report on Seaway Traffic, Potential and Existing Port Facilities, Port of Greater Detroit. Washington, 1956.

Jeffries, Edward J. Detroit's Critical Transportation Needs. Statement of Edward J. Jeffries, jr., Mayor of Detroit, Before the House Committee on Roads, . . . March 27, 1944. Detroit, 1944.

Kornhauser, Arthur W. Attitudes of Detroit People Toward Detroit; Summary of a Detailed Report. Detroit, 1952.

Kubota, Frank M., ed. Our Metropolitan Community, What Goals and Guidelines? A Community-wide Conference on Common Goals for the Six-County Metropolitan Detroit Area. . . . May 6, 1903. Detroit, 1903.

Library Service. vol. 1 - date. 1917/18 - date. Detroit, 1917 - date.

Miskouaki, Ottawa Chief. . . . Indian Affairs Around Detroit in 1706. Speech of Miskouaki, an Ottawa Chief to the Marquis Vaudreuil Governor General of Canada and his Reply, September, 1706. Trans. Col. Charles Whittlesey. in Western Reserve Historical Society. Historical and Archaeological Tracts. No. 8. Cleveland, 1871.

Mowitz, Robert J. and Deil S. Wright. Profile of a Metropolis, A Case Book. Detroit, 1962.

Munger, Thomas L. Detroit and World-Trade; A Survey of the City's Present and Potential Foreign Trade and Seaboard Traffic, and the Facilities Therefor with Special Reference to the Sea. . . . Detroit, 1920.

Quaife, Milo M., ed. The John Askin Papers. Detroit, 1928 - 1931. 2 vols.

The Municipal Code of the City of Detroit, 1936. Containing the City Charter. . . the Compiled Ordinances. . . Detroit, 1937.

Municipal Code. City of Detroit. Detroit, 1945.

Ordinances of the City. . . Revised and Published by Order of the Common Council. Detroit, 1864.

The Revised Charter and Ordinances of the City of Detroit. Detroit, 1848.

Report of the Street Railway Commission and the Rapid Transit Commission to Hon. John C. Lodge, Mayor, and the Honorable the Common Council on a Rapid Transit System for the City of Detroit, February 9, 1929. Detroit, 1929.

The Planner; Issued for the Detroit Plan Commission. 1934-date. Detroit, 1934 - date.

The Revised Ordinances of the City of Detroit for the Year 1871. . . . Detroit, 1871.

The Revised Ordinances of the City of Detroit for the Year 1878. . . . Detroit, 1878.

The Revised Ordinances of the City of Detroit for the Year 1884. . . . Detroit, 1884.

The Revised Ordinances of the City of Detroit for the Year 1895. . . . Detroit, 1895.

Welfare. February, 1959 - Date. Detroit, 1959 - date. Issued by the Detroit Public Welfare Department.

SECONDARY SOURCES

Asher, Cash. Sacred Cows, A Story of the Recall of Mayor Bowles. Detroit, 1931. An interesting analysis of the first recall attempt which succeeded in a large city in the United States.

Bald, Frederick C. Detroit's First American Decade, 1796-1805. Ann Arbor, Michigan, 1943. This is a fine study of the early years of Detroit's existence as an American town.

Barcus, Frank. All Around Detroit; A Narrative Pictorial History to Points of Interest. Detroit, 1939.

Beasley, Norman and Norman W. Stark. Made in Detroit.

New York, 1957. This is an account of two newspapermen who watched the city grow industrially. Many anecdotes are presented.

Bingay, Malcolm W. Detroit Is My Own Home Town. Indianapolis and New York, 1946. This is an enthusiastic account by a newspaperman who presents many yarns about the city.

Burton, Clarence M. "Cadillac's Village;" or "Detroit Under Cadillac." With a List of Property Owners and a History of the Settlement, 1701-1710. Detroit, 1916.

------------------. The City of Detroit, Michigan, 1701-1922. Detroit-Chicago, 1922. This is a detailed historical and biographical account of the major aspects of the development of the city into the third decade of the twentieth century.

------------------. Detroit in Earlier Days, A Few Notes on Some of the Old Buildings in the City. Detroit, 1918.

Carey, Albert B. Canadian-American Relations Along the Detroit River. Detroit, 1957.

Catlin, Albert B. The Story of Detroit. Detroit, 1923. This is an outline of Detroit's history which was originally a serial in the Detroit News.

Chikota, Richard A. and Michael C. Moran, ed. Riot in the Cities; An Analytical Symposium on the Causes and Effects. Fair Lawn, N. J., 1970. This work illustrates the basic aspects of riots, civil disobedience and centers on the 1967 Detroit riots.

Clark, Joe. Detroit, God's Greatest City. Detroit, 1962. This work illustrates the major attributes of the city.

Compendium of History and Biography of the City of Detroit and Wayne County, Michigan. . . Chicago, 1909.

Crathern, Alice Tarbell. In Detroit Courage Was the Fashion; The Contribution of Women to the Development of Detroit from 1701 to 1951. Detroit, 1953.

Dain, Floyd R. Detroit and the Westward Movement. Detroit, 1951.

The Detroit Historical Society, December 1921 - January

1952. A Chronicle, comp. under the direction of Gracie Brainerd Krumm. . . Detroit, 1952.

Detroit Michigan. Public Library. Antoine de la Mothe Cadillac and Detroit Before the Conspiracy of Pontiac. A Bibliography. Detroit, 1912.

Detroit News. Now and Later in Detroit. Detroit, 1944.

Detroit Public Library. Detroit In Its World Setting; A 250-Year Chronology, 1701-1951. Rae Elizabeth Rips, ed. Detroit, 1953.

Farmer, Silas. The History of Detroit and Michigan; or, The Metropolis Illustrated; A Chronological Cyclopaedia of the Past and Present, Including a Full Record of Territorial Days in Michigan, and the Annals of Wayne County. Detroit, 1864.

Ferman, Louis A. Death of a Newspaper: The Story of the Detroit Times. A Study of Job Dislocation Among the Newspaper Workers in a Depressed Labor Market. Kalamazoo, Michigan, 1963.

Ferry, W. Hawkins. The Buildings of Detroit; A History: A Centennial Publication. Detroit, 1969. This is a chronological survey of the city's architecture from the eighteenth century to the present.

Forster, Edith Caroline. Yesterday's Highways: Travelling Around Early Detroit. Detroit, 1951.

Freitag, Alfred J. Detroit in the Civil War. Detroit, 1951. This work concerns the contributions made by the citizens to the war effort.

Green, Jerry. Year of the Tiger; The Diary of Detroit's World Champions. New York, 1970. The author chronicles the manner in which the team captured the American League Pennant and won the World Series after a 23-year period between championships.

Greenstone, David. A Report on the Politics of Detroit. Cambridge, Mass., 1961.

Guderian, Haig. "Moral Sense" and Nightmare, 1957-1959. Detroit, 1959. This work concerns the Detroit Symphony Orchestra and its problems.

Hamlin, Marie Caroline Watson. Legends of Le Detroit. Detroit, 1884. Presents interesting anecdotes and tales of early Detroit.

Hanawalt, Leslie L. A Place of Light; the History of Wayne State University. Detroit, 1968. This is a history of the colleges which eventually combined to form the University.

Hersey, John. The Algiers Motel Incident. New York, 1968. The author centers on the shooting at the motel during the riots in Detroit. He interviewed the participants and examined police and court records.

Holli, Melvin G. Reform in Detroit: Hazen S. Pingree and Urban Politics. New York, 1969. This is a political biography of the four-term mayor indicating how he reformed many aspects of the city government.

Hough, John T., jr. A Peck of Salt; A Year in the Ghetto. New York, 1970. This is a chronicle of the author's service as a VISTA volunteer in Chicago and Detroit.

Hoult, Thomas Ford and Albert J. Mayer. The Population Revolution in Detroit. Detroit, 1963.

Hyshka, Dorian L. The Detroit Free Press: Motivation Research Looks at Detroit Newspaper Readers. Detroit, 1955.

Laut, Agnes Christina. Cadillac, Knight Errant of the Wilderness, Founder of Detroit, Governor of Louisiana from the Great Lakes to the Gulf. Indianapolis, 1931. This was the first biography of Antoine de la Mothe Cadillac, founder of Detroit.

Lee, Alfred M. and Norman D. Humphrey. Race Riot, Detroit, 1943. New York, 1968. This is a reprint of the work which gave a chronology of the events of the June 1943 riots. It indicated the failure of the city to cope with the situation effectively.

Lenski, Gerhard. The Religious Factor; A Sociological Study of Religion's Impact on Politics, Economics and Family Life. New York, 1962. This is a study of the various religious and racial groups and whether it determines an individual's political, economic and family life.

Lewis, Ferris E. Detroit; A Wilderness Outpost of Old France. Detroit, 1951. This is a study of the city's early history.

Lieb, Frederick George. The Detroit Tigers. New York, 1946. This work by the baseball writer gives a sketch of the players and management of the team as well as the growth of the town.

Lincoln, James H. Anatomy of a Riot: A Detroit Judge's Report. Detroit, 1969. This study indicates how juveniles were dealt with during the riots and also indicates some of the problems of the judiciary during the 1967 disturbances.

Lodge, John C. in collaboration with Milo M. Quaife. I Remember Detroit. Detroit, 1949.

Lovett, William Pierce. Detroit Rules Itself. Detroit, 1931. Shows how the city was able to reform its government and become one of the best run cities in America in the late 1920's and early 1930's.

Marquis, Albert N., ed. The Book of Detroiters; A Biographical Dictionary of Leading Men of the City of Detroit. 2nd rev. ed. Chicago, 1914.

Merchants' and Manufacturers' Exchange. Detroit in History and Commerce. . . . Detroit, 1891.

Metcalf, Kenneth N. Fun and Frolic in Early Detroit. Detroit, 1951. This is an interesting work showing how the colonists and early settlers of Detroit amused themselves.

Munger, Thomas. Detroit To-Day. A Brief History of Detroit's Origin and Development Emphasizing How the City's Growth Is Dependent on the Development of Adequate Transportation Facilities, and More Particularly the Great Lakes-St. Lawrence Route to the Atlantic Ocean. Detroit, 1921.

Paradise, Scott I. Detroit Industrial Mission, A Personal Narrative. New York, 1968. This journal of Rev. Paradise indicates how he and other clergymen who were concerned with the thought forms and technical structure of industry work out their ideas.

Parkins, Almon Ernest. . . . The Historical Geography of Detroit. . . . Chicago, 1918.

Polscher, Andrew A. Father Richard; Notes on His Printing in Early Detroit. Detroit, 1952.

Pound, Arthur. Detroit, Dynamic City. New York, 1940. Presents a good history of the city from the Indian sieges to the industrial era, emphasizing the early period.

Powell, Lyman Pierson, ed. Historical Towns of the Western States. New York, 1940. This is a fine study of many of the western cities including Detroit.

Quaife, Milo M. This Is Detroit; 1701-1951, Two Hundred and Fifty Years in Pictures. Detroit, 1951.

Radive, Floyd. Detroit; A French Village on the Frontier. Detroit, 1951.

Radio Staff of the Detroit News. "WWJ -- The Detroit News"; The History of Radio-Phone Broadcasting by the Earliest and Foremost of Newspaper Stations. . . Detroit, 1922.

Roberts, Robert Ellis. Sketches and Reminiscences of the City of the Straits and Its Vicinity. Detroit, 1884.

Ross, Robert B. and G. B. Catlin. Landmarks of Wayne County and Detroit. . . . Detroit, 1898.

Sauter, Van Gordon and Burleigh Hines. Nightmare in Detroit: A Rebellion and Its Victims. New York, 1968. These two newspapermen present an account of the disorders in 1967. The background comes from interviews with relatives and friends of the deceased.

Shogan, Robert and Tom Craig. The Detroit Race Riot; A Study in Violence. Chicago, 1964. This study of the 1943 riot indicates the various problems and the inept handling of the matter as compared with Mayor LaGuardia of New York.

"Sixty Years"; A Compilation of Articles Describing Six Decades in the Growth and Development of Detroit and Its Environs, 1881-1941. Originally Published in the Detroit Free Press During August, 1941, in Observance of Hudson's Sixtieth Jubilee Year. Detroit, 1941.

Stark, George W. City of Destiny, the Story of Detroit. Detroit, 1943. This is a fine analysis of the history and industrial potential of the City.

---------------. Seventy-five Years of Public Service: The Detroit News, the Home Newspaper. Detroit, 1948.

---------------. In Old Detroit. Detroit and New York, 1939.

Trowbridge, Charles Christopher. Detroit, Past and Present, in Relation to Its Social and Physical Condition. Detroit, 1864.

Upson, Lent Dayton. The Growth of a City Government, An Enumeration of Detroit's Municipal Activities. . . . Detroit, 1931.

Warner, Charles Forbes. Picturesque Detroit and Environs. 1,000 Illustrations. Northampton, Massachusetts, 1893.

White, Lee A. The Detroit News: Eighteen Hundred and Seventy-three - Nineteen Hundred and Seventeen, A Record of Progress. Detroit, 1918.

Wolf, Eleanor P. and Charles N. Lebeaux. Change and Renewal in An Urban Community; Five Case Studies in Detroit. New York, 1970. This is a study of five issues in the inner city: transition from white to black residency in a middle class integrated area; life styles and attitudes in a low-income black area; and urban renewal areas in relation to business and residence.

Woodford, Frank N. Parnassus on Main Street; A History of the Detroit Public Library. Detroit, 1966. Using the library's own records and files as well as other information the author presents an indepth chronological study of the development of the library.

ARTICLES

Catlin, George B. "The Regime of the Governor and Judges of Michigan Territory," Michigan History Magazine, vol. XV, Winter, 1931, pp. 19-41.

Delanglez, Jean. "The Genesis and Building of Detroit," Mid-America, April, 1948, pp. 75-104.

Dickie, James F. "Reminiscences of Detroit," Michigan History Magazine, vol. XIV, Fall, 1930, pp. 579-650.

Erichsen, Hugo. "My Memories of Old Detroit," Michigan History Magazine, vol. XVII, 1933, pp. 204-246, 281-325.

Havran, Martin J. "Windsor and Detroit Relations During the Civil War," Michigan History. vol. XXXVIII, December, 1954, pp. 371-389.

Horsman, Reginald, "Frontier Detroit, 1760- 1812," Michigan in Perspective. Occasional publication, no. 1. Detroit, 1964.

Hudgins, Bert. "Old Detroit; Drainage and Land Farms," Michigan History, vol. XXX, June, 1940, pp. 348-368.

McLean, Robert Craik. "Detroit, The Industrial City," Western Architect, vol. XXIV, 1916, pp. 129-136.

Minas, Thomas. "The Detroit Bank, The First Bank in the Territory of Michigan, Incorporated at Detroit, September 19, 1806," Massachusetts Historical Society Proceedings, Series 2, vol. XX, 1907, pp. 521-525.

Petersen, Eugene T. "The Civil War Comes to Detroit," Detroit Historical Society Bulletin, vol. XVII, Summer, 1961.

Rankin, Lois. "Detroit Nationality Groups," Michigan History Magazine, vol. XXIII, 1939, pp. 129-211.

Reibel, Daniel B. "A Kind of Citadel, 1764-1805," Michigan History. vol. XLVII, March, 1963, pp. 47-71.

Sitkoff, Harvard. "The Detroit Race Riot of 1943," Michigan History, vol. LIII, Fall, 1969, pp. 183-206.

Stratton, William B. "The Growth of Detroit," Western Architect, vol. XXIV, 1916, pp. 126-128.